E-LEARNING
Uncovered!_{SM}

Adobe
Captivate
5.5

Diane Elkins
Desirée Pinder

E-Learning Uncovered: Adobe Captivate 5.5

By Diane Elkins and Desirée Pinder

Alcorn, Ward, & Partners, Inc. dba Artisan E-Learning

2771-29 Monument Road #329

Jacksonville, FL 32225

www.artisanelearning.com

Trademarks

Adobe Captivate is a registered trademarks of Adobe Systems Incorporated.

Other product and company names mentioned herein may be trademarks of their respective owners. Use of trademarks or product names is not intended to convey endorsement or affiliation in this book.

Warning and Disclaimer

The information provided is on an "as is" basis. Every effort has been made to make this book as complete and as accurate as possible, but no warranty or fitness is implied. The authors and the publisher shall have neither liability nor responsibility to any person or entity with respect to any loss or damages arising from the information contained in this book.

Table of Contents

Table of Contents

Table of Contents

Introduction

It all started with a free steak dinner. Back in 2003, a client and I were speaking at an industry conference. As presenters, we were invited to a reception sponsored by some company we'd never heard of...eHelp. "It's a free steak dinner," we thought. "Why not?" That's when I was first introduced to Captivate (then called RoboDemo). Little did I know that the seemingly inconsequential decision of where to have dinner nine years ago would culminate in the publishing of this book. I've been using RoboDemo/Captivate ever since—and I even still have the t-shirt from that night.

Over the years, Captivate has evolved. Software simulations started out as its bread and butter. But with each new release, the makers (eHelp, then Macromedia, then Adobe) have added more and more features to make it a full-blown e-learning authoring tool, suitable for any type of training content. In recent years, users have been given access to many new building blocks that allow for custom logic such as actions and variables to create conditional logic. Its simplicity and complexity mean you can be recording screen captures in just a few minutes, yet still be learning about new things you can do with it years later.

In this book, we've created a road map for you to follow. However, there's no one way to get to where you want to go. Learn the capabilities and the building blocks, and then see where they take you. You'll notice a lot of cross-references in this book because of how all the features are interrelated. Enjoy practicing, exploring, and creating.

Acknowledgments

Desirée and I would like to extend our special thanks to some of the many people who made this book possible. We'd like to thank our extended production team of Judy Unrein, Amy Morrisey, and Nick Elkins. Allen Partridge, Chandranath Bhattacharya, and Akshay Bharadwaj—all from Adobe—rearranged their schedules during a very busy time to help answer some of our detailed technical questions. We also appreciate Marty Deutsch for reviewing an early draft and making some useful suggestions. And special thanks goes to Steve Elkins who helped me stay focused and motivated, kept me well-fed during the big deadlines, and found more than his share of missing commas.

Diane Elkins

Getting the Most Out of This Book

This book assumes you are a functional user of Windows software. If you are familiar with how to use dialog boxes, drop-down menus, and other standard Windows conventions, then you'll be fine. The book is written for the PC version of Captivate. If you are using Captivate for Mac, you'll still get a lot out of this book, but you may find some differences in some of the procedures. The Appendix has a few quick tips for Mac users.

Use the detailed table of contents and comprehensive index to help you find what you are looking for. In addition to procedures, look for all the hints, tips, and cautions that can help you save time, avoid problems, and make your courses more engaging.

 ## DESIGN TIP

Design Tips give you insight on how to implement the different features and include everything from graphic design to instructional design to usability.

 ## CAUTION

Pay special attention to the Cautions (which are full of "lessons learned the hard way") so you can avoid some common problems.

 ## BRIGHT IDEA

Bright Ideas are special explanations and ideas for getting more out of the software.

 ## POWER TIP

Power Tips are advanced tips and secrets that can help you take your production to the next level.

 ## TIME SAVER

Time Savers...well...save you time. These tips include software shortcuts and ways to streamline your production efforts.

 Web Resource:
Go to www.e-learninguncovered.com for related resources such as printable reference guides and screencasts.

 This symbol indicates a cross-reference to another part of the book.

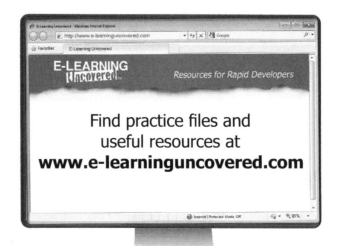

Find practice files and useful resources at
www.e-learninguncovered.com

Getting to Know Captivate

Adobe Captivate is an e-learning development tool with two main purposes: simulating computer procedures and creating non-simulation computer content.

For example, you might be creating a course on how to use a new time and attendance software program. You can use Captivate to:

- Record your desktop while you are performing the steps so that your students can sit back and watch the procedure being performed.

- Record your desktop while you are performing the steps and convert it to an interactive practice where the students get to perform the steps and get feedback.

- Create several screens of content with text, images, and media that cover business rules such as the leave-request policies, the approval workflow, and important deadlines.

- Build a quiz that tests the students on the key business rules.

In some ways, it is like getting two software packages in one. The difference between computer simulations and other content is important, as you'll use key features of the software differently based on the type of content you are working with.

Adobe Captivate can be used alone or in conjunction with other software packages. For example, you might:

- Create a single simulation or quiz in Captivate and publish it as a course.

- Create a series of simulations, and publish them all together as a single course.

- Create a series of simulations and embed each one into a web page, a help file, or a course created in a different authoring tool.

- Export your simulations to Adobe Flash to add custom programming.

Captivate can be purchased alone or as part of the Adobe eLearning Suite. Some features in the software are only available if you have the full eLearning Suite.

Notes

The Captivate Interface

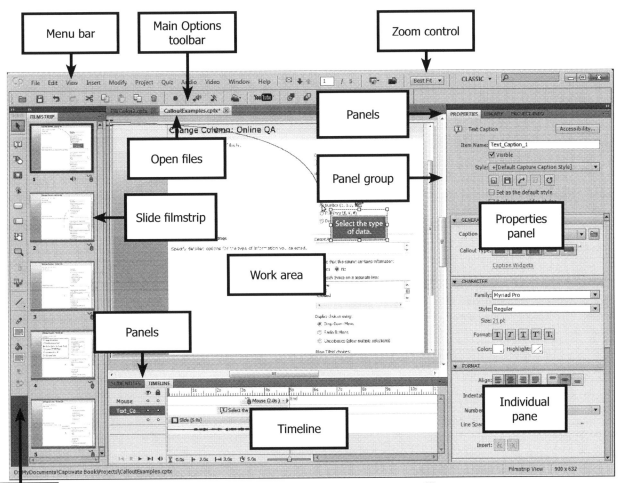

Menu bar

Main Options toolbar

Zoom control

Panels

Open files

Panel group

Properties panel

Slide filmstrip

Work area

Panels

Timeline

Individual pane

Object toolbar

 Appendix: Mac Interface, p. 219

Primary Menus & Toolbars

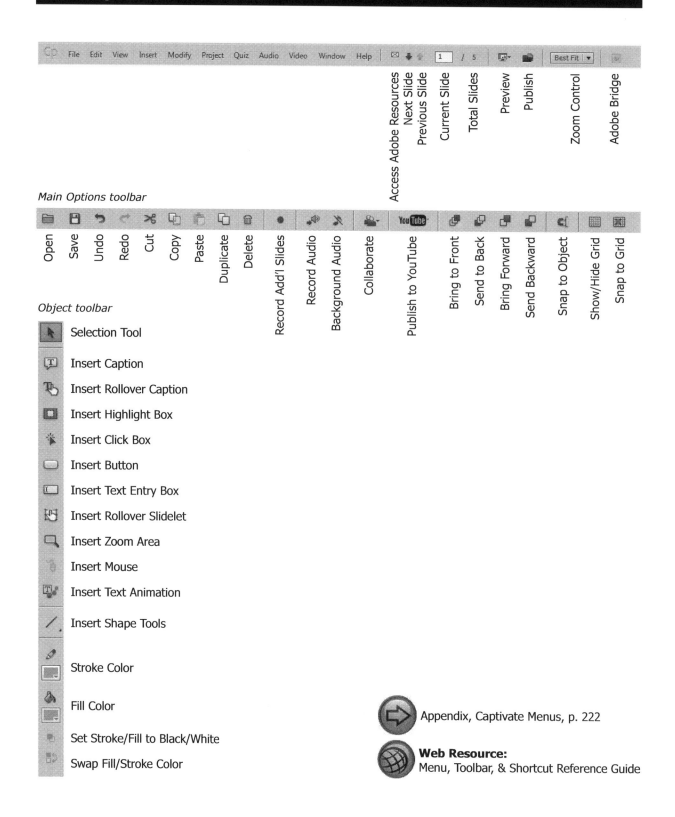

File   Edit   View   Insert   Modify   Project   Quiz   Audio   Video   Window   Help

- Access Adobe Resources
- Next Slide
- Previous Slide
- Current Slide
- Total Slides
- Preview
- Publish
- Zoom Control
- Adobe Bridge

Main Options toolbar

- Open
- Save
- Undo
- Redo
- Cut
- Copy
- Paste
- Duplicate
- Delete
- Record Add'l Slides
- Record Audio
- Background Audio
- Collaborate
- Publish to YouTube
- Bring to Front
- Send to Back
- Bring Forward
- Send Backward
- Snap to Object
- Show/Hide Grid
- Snap to Grid

Object toolbar

Selection Tool

Insert Caption

Insert Rollover Caption

Insert Highlight Box

Insert Click Box

Insert Button

Insert Text Entry Box

Insert Rollover Slidelet

Insert Zoom Area

Insert Mouse

Insert Text Animation

Insert Shape Tools

Stroke Color

Fill Color

Set Stroke/Fill to Black/White

Swap Fill/Stroke Color

Appendix, Captivate Menus, p. 222

Web Resource:
Menu, Toolbar, & Shortcut Reference Guide

Customize the Interface

You can customize the Captivate interface to best fit your needs and working styles.

To show or hide a toolbar or panel:
1. Go to the **Window** menu. **(A)**
2. Select or de-select the element you want to show or hide.

To expand or collapse a panel group:
- Click the double-arrows in the top corner of the group. **(B)**

To close a panel:
1. Click the icon in the upper-left corner of the panel. **(C)**
2. Select **Close** to close just that panel, or select **Close Group** to close all panels in that group.

To move a panel:
- Click and drag the tab with the panel name to the place where you want it. **(D)**

To move a whole panel group:
- Click and drag the dark gray bar for the group. **(E)**

To change the order of panels in a given group:
- Click and drag the tab left or right to the place where you want it. **(D)**

To expand or collapse panes within a panel:
- Click the arrow on the left side of the pane heading. **(F)**

To move a toolbar:
- Click and drag the double-dotted line to the place where you want it. **(G)**

BRIGHT IDEA

When moving panels and toolbars, look for a subtle blue highlight as you approach other panes or the edge of the interface. If you release the toolbar or panel when there is a blue highlight showing, that item will be "docked" in place. If there is no highlight showing, the panel or toolbar will be free floating.

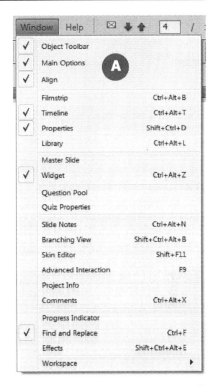

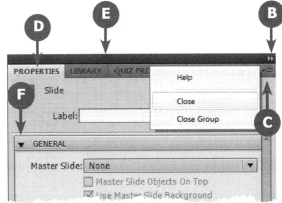

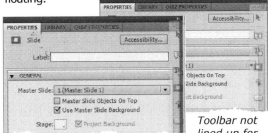

Toolbar being docked on the right ^

Toolbar not lined up for docking

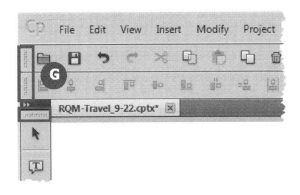

Customize the Interface (continued)

To change the width or height of panel:

1. Hover your mouse over the panel border until you see the double-headed arrow. **(A)**
2. Click and drag the border to the size you want.

To change the size of the thumbnails in the Filmstrip:

1. Right-click a thumbnail.
2. Select **Filmstrip**.
3. Select the size you want. **(B)**

To change the magnification of the slide in the work area:

1. Click the zoom drop-down menu. **(C)**
2. Select the magnification option you want.

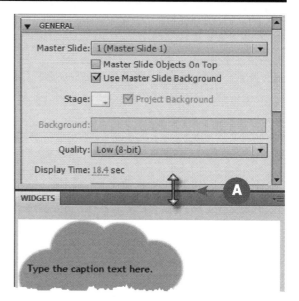

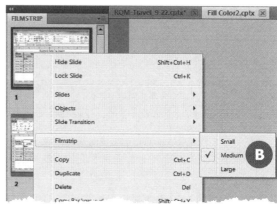

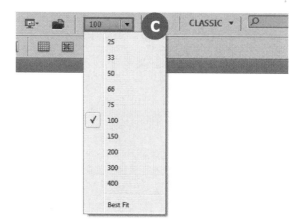

Customize the Interface (continued)

Workspaces

Workspaces are saved interface configurations. Captivate comes with several pre-made workspaces that are optimized for different functions. Each workspace has different panels showing or hidden based on what is needed for a given task. In addition, you can save your own workspaces to fit your needs. For example, if you can create a workspace with the **Slide Notes** showing if you plan to use closed captioning.

To apply an existing workspace:

1. Click the **Workspace** drop-down menu.
2. Select the workspace you want.

To create your own workspace:

1. Configure the toolbars and panels the way you want them.
2. Click the **Workspace** drop-down menu.
3. Select **New Workspace**.
4. Enter a name for the workspace.
5. Click **OK**.

Additional Workspace Options

Select **Manage Workspace** from the drop-down menu if you want to rename or delete any workspaces that you have created.

If you made changes to a workspace and want to go back to the original state, select the **Reset** option on the drop-down menu.

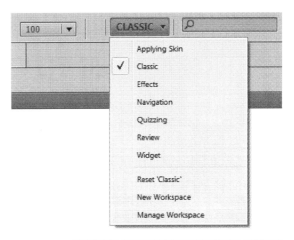

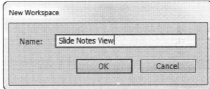

Open an Existing Project

To open Captivate:
1. Click the **Start** menu.
2. Select **All Programs**.
3. Select **Adobe Captivate 5.5**.

When you open Captivate, the **Welcome** screen appears, which has many of the same options as the **File** menu.

To open a project from the Welcome screen:
1. Select the file from the **Open Recent Item** list.

-or-

1. Click the **Open** link.
2. Find and select the file you want.
3. Click **Open**.

To open a project from the File menu:
1. Click the **File** menu.
2. Select **Open**.
3. Find and select the file you want.
4. Click **Open**.

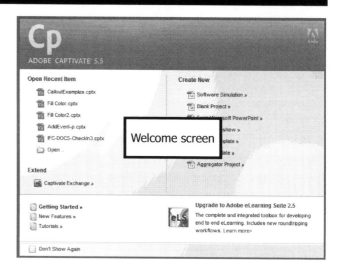

 CAUTION

When you launch Captivate, you may receive a warning saying some features may not be available unless you have administrator privileges. If your computer has security restrictions on it, some features *may* not work, depending on your particular restrictions. If you encounter problems, check with your I.T. department to get administrator priviledges on the computer, and then run Captivate as an administrator. To run as an administrator, right-click **Adobe Captivate 5.5** on the **Start** menu, and select **Run as Administrator**.

Moving Around a Project

Use any of the following methods to move around a project.

- Select a thumbnail in the **Filmstrip** to go to that slide. **(A)**
- Use your **Page Up** and **Page Down** keys move up or down one slide.
- Use the **Next Slide** and **Previous Slide** buttons to move up or down one slide. **(B)**
- Type a slide number in the field next to the arrows to jump to that slide. **(C)**

If you have more than one project open, you can move from project to project by clicking the tabs just above the work area. **(D)**

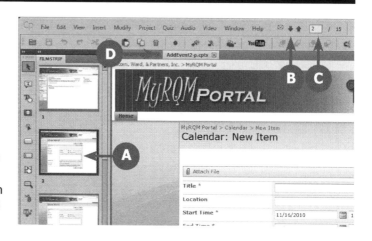

Save a Project

Options for saving a project:
- Click the **Save** button on the **Main Object** toolbar.
- Go to the **File** menu, and select **Save**.
- Press **Ctrl + S**.

Other saving options:
- Go to the **File** menu, and select **Save As** to save the file under a different name or in a different location.
- Click **Save All** on the **File** menu to save all open projects.

 CAUTION

Captivate versions are not backwards compatible. Projects saved in version 5.5 cannot be opened in previous versions. Files from previous versions can be opened in 5.5, but be careful, because you may not be able to open them again in the previous version––even if you don't even save them.

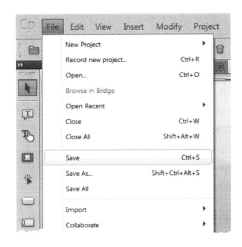

Close a Project

Options for closing a project:
- Go to the **File** menu, and select **Close** to close the current project.
- Go to the **File** menu, and select **Close All** to close all open projects.
- Click the **X** in the tab for a project. **(A)**
- Click the red **X** to close Captivate completely. **(B)**

The Properties Panel

Every object on your slide has properties: the mouse, captions, audio, etc. These properties are displayed and modified in the **Properties** panel. You will learn more about specific properties for each type of object in their respective chapters. Here are a few guidelines that apply to the **Properties** panel for any object type.

- If the **Properties** panel isn't showing, go to the **Window** menu, and select **Properties**.
- Select an object to view and change its properties.
- Select more than one object to view and change all shared properties.
- The options in the **Properties** panel will vary based on the item or object you have selected.
- Click the arrow next to the name of a pane to expand or collapse that pane. **(A)**
- Click the **Collapse to Icons** button to minimize the panel. **(B)**
- Click the drop-down menu in the top corner to close the panel. **(C)**
- In blue, underlined number fields, known as hot text, either click and type a new number, or click and drag left or right to increase or decrease the number. **(D)**

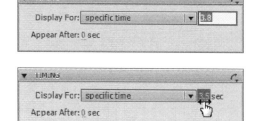

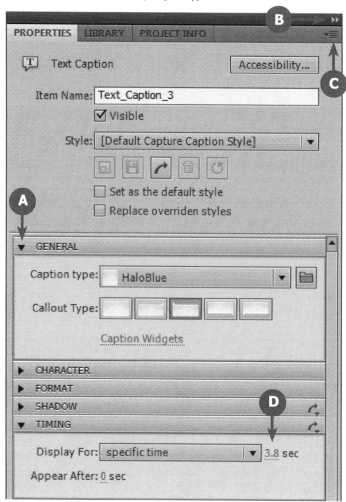

Objects and the Timeline

When you place an object on a slide, a corresponding line item is added to the Timeline. Among other things, you can adjust:

- **Layering**: Objects at the top of the **Timeline** appear in front of objects at the bottom of the **Timeline**.
- **Visibility**: Click the "eyeball" icon next to an object to hide it from view while working. (This does not affect your published movie, just what shows in the work area.)
- **Start Time and Length**: When the slide plays, objects appear when the "bar" for that object starts and disappear when the bar for that object ends.

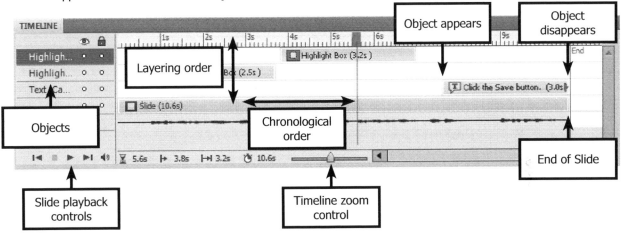

Object Properties, ch. 6
Timing Objects, p. 105

Preview a Project

To preview an individual slide:

1. Click the **Play** button in the **Timeline**. **(A)**

   -or-

1. Click the **Preview** button. **(B)**
2. Select **Play Slide**.

To preview more than one slide:

1. Click the **Preview** button.
2. Select the slide range you want.

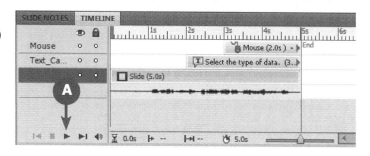

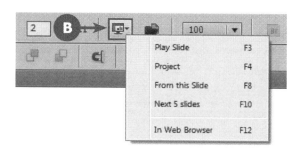

CAUTION

When you preview just a single slide, certain elements may not play properly, such as full-motion recording or certain highlight boxes. Previewing more than one slide at a time gives you a more representative view of what your project will look like when published.

BRIGHT IDEAS

- If you like to preview your project in chunks, you can change the **Next 5 slides** option to the number of slides you prefer to work with. For example, you might prefer to view 3 slides at a time. Go to the **Edit** menu, select **Preferences**, and click the **Defaults** category to change this option.

- With a regular preview, you have to close the preview to go back to your project and make changes. But if you choose the browser preview option, you can have the preview up in your browser window and your slides in the Captivate window, making it easier to switch between reviewing and editing.

- Be sure to learn the keyboard shortcuts for previewing, as these are big time savers!

Appendix: Useful Keyboard Shortcuts, p. 224

Creating New Projects

2

Because Captivate is such a versatile tool, there are several different types of projects you can create. In this chapter, you will learn how to create the primary project types. In the Special Tools and Wizards chapter (chapter 11), you will learn about some of the more specialized project types.

Primary Project Types

Blank Project: Create a blank project when you want to build a lesson from scratch and add slides and elements individually. (You can also add blank slides to any project.)

Project From MS PowerPoint: Create a new project from an existing PowerPoint presentation, where each slide in PowerPoint becomes a slide in your Captivate project. (You can also add individual PowerPoint slides to any project.)

Image Slideshow: Create a new project from a series of images, where each image becomes a slide in your project. (You can also add individual image slides to any project.)

Software Simulation: Create a project by recording what you do on your computer, creating either a sit-back-and-watch demonstration or an interactive try-it-yourself practice.

Special Project Types (covered in chapter 11)

Project Template: Create a template that includes slides, objects and object placeholders, settings, etc. to be used over and over again.

Project From Template: Create a new project based on a saved template.

Aggregator Project: Create a new project that combines existing movies. For example, if you have five simulations and five practices to teach a new time reporting system, you can combine and publish them all as a single course.

Mobile Project: If you have the Adobe eLearning Suite, create a mobile-friendly project using Adobe Device Central.

Multi-SCORM Packager: Create a course from multiple projects that integrates with a Learning Management System.

In this chapter:
- Blank Projects
- PowerPoint Projects
- Image Slideshows
- Software Simulations
- Recording Settings & Preferences

Notes

Create a New, Blank Project

To create a new, blank project:

1. Select **Blank Project** on the **Welcome** screen.

    - or -

1. Go to the **File** menu.

2. Select **New** Project.

3. Select **Blank** Project.

4. Enter the dimensions for your project from the drop-down menu or by manually entering the dimensions.

5. Click **OK**.

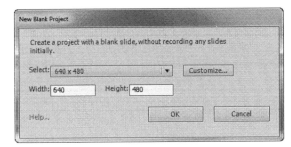

Adding PowerPoint Content

Rather than building your slides in Captivate, you can import existing content from Microsoft PowerPoint. Slide notes, audio, and some animations carry over to the Captivate slide. Slide notes go into the **Slide Notes** panel in Captivate, audio is added as an audio object in the **Timeline**, and certain types of animations (both automatic and on-click) will work in Captivate as well. You can edit the PowerPoint slides right from Captivate (assuming you have PowerPoint installed on that computer) and even link your project to the PowerPoint document to make sure you are working with the latest information.

You can either create a new project from PowerPoint or add individual slides to an existing project. In either case, one slide is created in Captivate for each imported slide from PowerPoint.

Create a New Project From PowerPoint

To create a new project from PowerPoint:

1. Select **From Microsoft PowerPoint** on the **Welcome** screen.

   - or -

1. Go to the **File** menu.
2. Select **New Project**.
3. Select **Project From MS PowerPoint**.
4. Find and select the file you want.
5. Click **Open**.
6. Enter the properties you want.
7. Click **OK**.

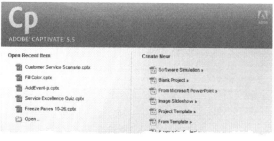

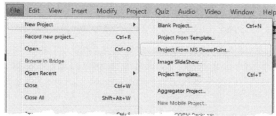

PowerPoint Import Properties

Project Properties

This section is only available when creating a new project from PowerPoint. If you are importing slides into an existing project, then the project's properties will be used.

Name: The name of the PowerPoint file is used as the default name for the project. You can change the name here if you want to.

Width, Height, and Preset Sizes: Either select a preset size from the menu or enter in your own values for the size of the project. The default size is the size of your PowerPoint presentation.

Maintain Aspect Ratio: Check this box if you want the project to have the same proportion as the PowerPoint slides. This prevents the images from being stretched in one direction or the other.

Slide Preview: Check or uncheck the box **(A)** for each slide to indicate which slides you want to import. To save time, use the **Select All** and **Clear All** buttons.

Advance Slide: Indicate if you want the slides to advance automatically on the **Timeline** (like any other slide in your project) or advance on mouse click. If you select the mouse click option, Captivate includes a click box that covers each slide. That way, when the student clicks anywhere on the slide, the slide advances, just like it would in PowerPoint.

Linked: When this box is checked **(B)**, Captivate links to the PowerPoint file instead of embedding it into the presentation. This makes your project size smaller, but it also means you have to have access to the PowerPoint file to edit the project. In addition, if you link the file, any edits you make to the slide in Captivate are made to the original PowerPoint file as well—which you may or may not want.

With a linked file, slide labels, slide notes, and audio files are brought in on the initial import, but are not updated if changes are made later.

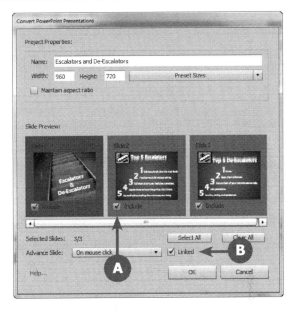

Import Individual PowerPoint Slides, p. 31
Edit a PowerPoint Slide, p. 32
Update an Imported Slide, p. 33

DESIGN TIP

The default size for a PowerPoint presentation is 960 x 720. If you know you will be importing PowerPoint slides, you might want to either make your Captivate file that big, or adjust your PowerPoint page size to be the same as your Captivate project size.

CAUTION

- Students may not know that they are supposed to click on the slide to trigger an animation or advance to the next slide. Make sure you include clear instructions.

- With a linked file, make sure the PPT file stays in the same location with the same file name. Otherwise, the link between the two will be broken.

- Avoid editing both versions of a slide at once (the PPT slide and the linked Captivate slide) as your edits might not be saved properly.

Link when you want to...	**Embed** when you want to...
• Keep the file size small. • Update the PPT when you update the Captivate slide.	• Work with the project even if you don't have access to the PowerPoint file. • Import a PowerPoint file that is likely to change locations. • Make changes to the Captivate slide without changing the original PPT file.

Image Slideshow and Images

There are three ways to add images to your projects:

- **New image slideshow**: Select a folder of images and create a new project with each selected image on its own slide. Use this for a quick and easy slideshow.

- **Image slide**: Add an image slide to every project, with the image as the background.

- **Image on slide**: Place an image on any existing slide and either keep it as a slide object that can be moved, resized, and manipulated, or merge it to become part of the background.

Adding Image Slides, p. 34
Adding Images to a Slide, p. 54

Create a New Image Slideshow

To create a new image slideshow:

1. Select **Image Slideshow** on the **Welcome** screen.

   - or -

1. Go to the **File** menu.

2. Select **New Project**.

3. Select **Image SlideShow**.

4. Select a preset size from the menu or enter in your own values for the size of the project.

5. Click the **OK** button.

6. Find and select the images you want to add.

7. Click the **OK** button.

If your images are larger than the dimensions for the project, you get a dialog box after step 5 that gives you options for resizing the image as well as image editing tools.

Resizing Options

Fit to Stage: This option shrinks the image to the largest size that will fit fully on the page. Because the aspect ratio (height/width proportion) may be different on the image than on the slide, you may end up with empty space either above and below or to the left and right of the image.

Crop: This option lets you crop off some of the picture for a better fit. Drag the crop frame handles and move the crop frame to indicate the part of the image you want to keep. That portion of the image will then appear as large as possible on the slide.

Constrain Proportions: If you are cropping the image, check this box to make the crop frame the same aspect ratio as the slide. Uncheck it if you want to be able to change the aspect ratio.

Apply to All: Click this button if you want to use the same sizing approach for all pictures being imported. If you do not want to treat them all the same, click the arrows at the bottom of the screen to move from picture to picture, adjusting each one individually.

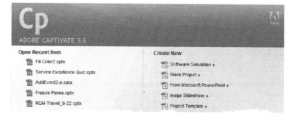

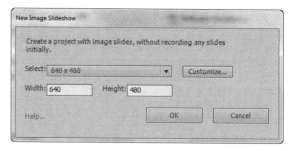

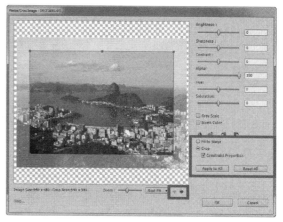

Software Simulations

Software simulations, also known as screen recordings, let you capture whatever you are doing on your computer. You can create two different types of simulations: sit-back-and-watch demonstrations, and interactive try-it-yourself practices where the student gets to perform the steps and get feedback.

Preparing for a Screen Recording Session

There are many things you'll need to plan and do before you even open up Captivate, both in your computer settings and in the software you plan to capture. To help ensure you get a good, clean capture, use this checklist before you click the **Record** button.

- ❏ Create sample files, scenarios, etc., to demonstrate during the capture. For example, if you are demonstrating how to approve a timesheet, you will need to submit an employee timesheet and make sure your sample supervisor is set up to receive that timesheet.

- ❏ Walk through all the steps you plan to demonstrate. You'd be surprised at how many times this helps you realize you weren't sure about a step or you need to do some more prep work.

- ❏ Undo anything you did during the walk-through. For example, if you walked through the steps for authorizing a timesheet, you might need to go back and unauthorize it for the actual capture.

- ❏ Position your application window so any drop-down menus stay within the recording area. Usually, moving the window to the edge of your monitor helps with this. It may force the drop-down menu to reposition itself.

- ❏ Turn up your volume so you can hear the camera shutter sound.

- ❏ Turn off email, instant messenger, and any other application that might generate an unwanted pop-up window while you are in the middle of a capture.

- ❏ If you are switching back and forth between demo and practice modes, double-check to make sure you change the mode to record the way you want.

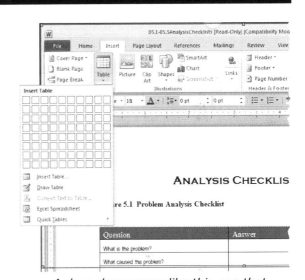

A drop-down menu like this one that extends beyond your recording window can cause havoc during a recording session.

Record a Software Simulation

To record a software simulation:

1. Open the application you wish to record.

2. On the **Welcome** screen, click **Software Simulation (A)**, or go to the **New** menu and select **Record New Project**.

3. Configure the recording settings (covered in the remainder of the chapter). **(B)**

4. Adjust the red recording frame that appears around the application being recorded, if needed.

5. Click the **Record** button. **(C)**

6. Perform the steps of the procedure you are demonstrating.

7. Press the **End** button on your keyboard or click the **Captivate** icon in your system tray.

 Web Resource:
Screencast: Setting Up and Recording

Recording Size Settings

Screen Area: This option lets you designate the pixel size of the capture and then manually resize the application to fit in the red recording frame.

    Custom Size: Enter the pixel dimensions you want your recording to be, or select from one of the presets in the drop-down menu. Use the **Customize** button to add your own presets if there is a certain dimension you use regularly.

    Full Screen: This option records everything on your entire monitor. If you have more than one monitor, you can pick which one you want to record.

Application: Use this option to have the recording frame automatically size itself to the application.

    Application Drop-Down Menu: Select the application you want to record. The menu shows all open applications.

    Snap to: Application Window: The recording frame snaps to the application at its current size.

    Snap to: Application Region: The recording frame snaps to a specific region of the application, such as the toolbars across the top. Move your mouse around the application until the recording frame "finds" the region you want to record.

    Snap to: Custom Size: You can enter a custom pixel dimension, and the application snaps to fit those dimensions.

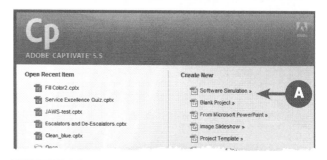

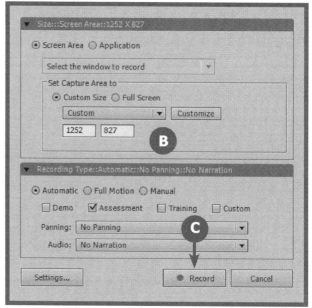

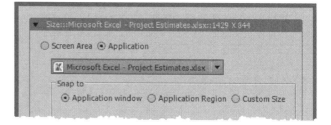

 BRIGHT IDEA

Snap to: Custom Size gives you the most control and consistency. You enter the size, so you know it will look right in the final published course. Because the application snaps to the frame instead of your manually sizing it, there's no risk that you'll be off by a few pixels. This is useful if you have to go back later and re-record more frames, as everything will look consistent.

Recording Settings

Recording Type Settings

Automatic: Captivate automatically takes captures when you perform certain steps, such as mouse clicks and keystrokes, as well as when the system performs certain functions, such as displaying a warning.

You can record in up to four modes at once, based on which boxes are checked at the time of recording. You can customize each by clicking the **Settings** button, which is covered on the next page.

> **Demo**: Use this for a sit-back-and-watch lesson of the procedure—good for introducing the procedure and explaining all of the variations, hints, tips, etc.
>
> **Assessment**: Use this to test the students' knowledge as they perform every step themselves, with scoring for every step and the option to limit the number of attempts.
>
> **Training**: Use this to help students practice the procedure themselves, providing feedback but not grading their success.
>
> **Custom**: Use this method for completely custom recording settings.
>
> For this book, any simulation in which the student performs the steps (assessment, training, and some custom settings) will be called a practice.

Full Motion: In this mode, everything you do is recorded in real time as a video. This is useful if you have a lot of dragging actions, such as resizing a graphic, or if there are subtle elements you want to show, such as rollover effects. (In **Automatic** mode, full-motion recording is used, but only for certain actions such as scrolling or dragging.)

Manual: All captures are done manually by you when you press the **Print Screen** key. You might use this if you just want an overview of the main screens, rather than showing every single step. (In **Automatic** mode, you can manually add a screen capture at any time with the **Print Screen** key.)

Panning: By default, panning is turned off, meaning the red recording frame is fixed in one place during the recording. You can also choose **Automatic Panning**, which moves the red recording frame around automatically if your mouse goes outside of the frame. **Manual Panning** lets you move the recording frame around manually during the recording.

Audio: By default, audio is not recorded during capture. If you want to record audio while you capture, select a microphone from the menu.

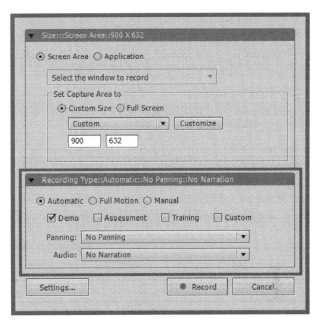

 DESIGN TIP

You can save time by recording in several modes at once. However, it is less challenging to the student if the practice exercise is exactly the same as the demonstration. Consider having a separate practice to introduce variations of the procedure. For example, if the demo is of someone entering a day of vacation on Tuesday, you may want a practice of someone entering a sick day on Wednesday.

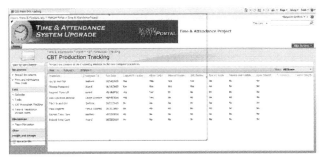

With a wide application like this, it might be useful to use panning, rather than reduce the size to fit in the red recording area.

Change Recording Preferences

To change recording preferences:

1. Click the **Settings** button in the recording window.

   - or -

1. Go to the **Edit** menu and select **Preferences**.

2. In the **Category** pane, select the category for the settings you want to work with.

3. Make the changes you want.

4. Click the **OK** button.

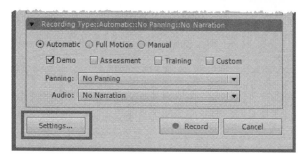

Recording Settings Category

Generate Captions In: If you are using automatic recording to create captions, use this menu to select a language other than English for the captions.

Audio Options

> **Narration**: Check this if you want to record narration into a microphone while you are recording.

> **Actions in Real Time**: Check this if you want to record the steps at their actual speed.

> **Camera Sounds**: During recording, a camera shutter sound plays every time a capture is taken. This lets you know if you are getting the captures you need. Uncheck this box if you don't want those sounds. (The sounds are not included in the finished movie.)

> **Keystrokes**: When you type during a capture, Captivate captures each keystroke. Uncheck this box if you don't want individual keystrokes captured, but just want the typed passage to appear at once.

> **Hear Keyboard Tap Sounds**: During recording, a tap sound plays for each key you type. Uncheck this box if you don't want to hear these sounds. (There is a separate option in **Publish Settings** for including keystroke sounds in the published movie.)

Hide

> **Recording Window:** Check if you don't want to see the red recording frame.

> **Task Icon**: Check to hide the icon during recording.

> **System Tray Icon**: Check to hide the system tray icon **(A)** during recording.

Move New Windows Inside Recording Area: If another window opens during a capture, such as a dialog box, the pop-up window will be moved into the red recording area, unless you uncheck this box.

Automatically Use FMR for: During automatic recording, full-motion recording (FMR) is triggered every time you use a dragging action or use a mouse wheel. Uncheck these boxes if you don't want full-motion recording to trigger automatically.

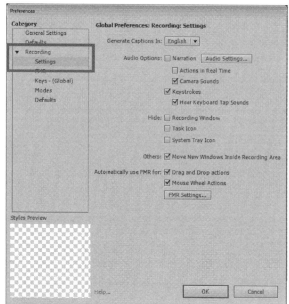

 Working with Audio, chapter 5

 CAUTION

If you are recording audio while you are capturing, then be sure to turn off the options for camera sounds and keyboard tap sounds. Otherwise, they'll get recorded with your voiceover!

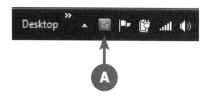

Recording Preferences (continued)

FMR Category (Full-Motion Recording)

Show Mouse in Full Motion Recording Mode:
By default, the mouse is included in any full-motion recording. Uncheck this box if you don't want the mouse recorded. For example, you might want a recording of some sort of animation and wouldn't want the mouse in the way.

Working Folder: The full-motion recording is saved as a SWF file and is included in your capture. This field indicates where that file will be stored, and can be changed by clicking the **Browse** button.

SWF Conversion: You can select the video setting for any FMR. **16 bit** creates a smaller file size, but the fewer number of available colors may affect your quality. **32 bit** gives you more colors, but will create a larger file.

FMR Mode: Use this slider to adjust the quality setting for the FMR portion of your captures. **Video** has the highest quality settings and therefore the highest file size. **Smaller SWF Size** has the lowest quality setting and lowest file size. The **Safe** option uses your system resources to determine what settings to use.

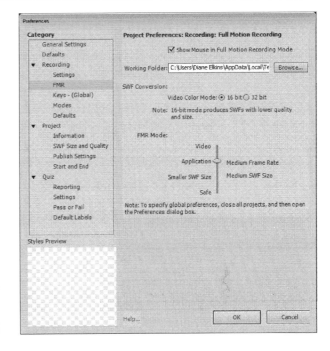

Keys Category

This category displays the various keyboard shortcuts that can be used during recording. If you want to change any of them, just click in a field and type the shortcut you want to use instead. For example, you may be taking a capture of an application that uses some of these function keys. In these cases, you'd want to change the shortcut in Captivate so it doesn't create a conflict.

 CAUTION

The **Print Screen** key is the default for manually capturing a screen in both Captivate and Snagit. If you have Snagit installed on your computer and press **Print Screen** during a capture, it may launch Snagit. You'll want to change the hotkey for manual captures in either Captivate or in Snagit to avoid a conflict during your capture session.

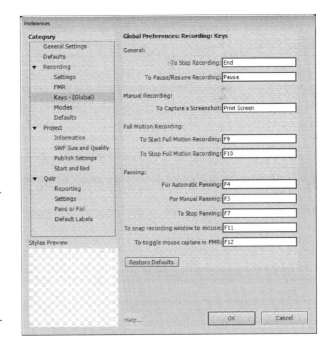

 **Web Resource:**
Style Guide Template

Recording Preferences (continued)

Modes Category

In the **Modes** category, you can configure the settings for each of the four automatic recording modes. First, select the mode you want to configure from the drop-down menu at the top **(A)**, and then make any changes you want for that mode.

Captions

Add Text Captions: Captivate automatically adds captions to your steps, e.g., "Click the **OK** button."

Convert Tooltips to Rollover Captions: If your software has tooltips (small captions that give the name of the tool when you hover over it), Captivate creates a similar rollover caption for you.

Mouse

Show Mouse Location and Movement: Captivate includes the mouse and a streamlined path in the capture (smooth path from one click to the next rather than the actual path the mouse took).

Add Highlight Boxes on Click: Captivate adds a highlight box around the button, menu, etc. that you click. This can provide visual emphasis, and also makes it easy to create job aids using the **Publish to Print** publishing option.

The default settings for **Demonstration** mode (shown below) include captions, mouse movement, and highlight boxes. The default settings for the two practice modes (**Training** and **Assessment**) do not include these objects, but instead, include the interactive elements covered on the next page.

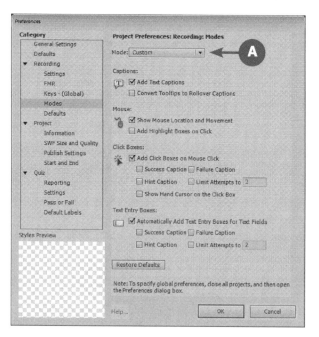

 CAUTION

This dialog box only changes the settings for each mode, NOT which mode you will actually be recording in. That is determined by the check boxes in the recording window.

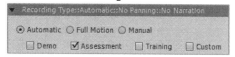

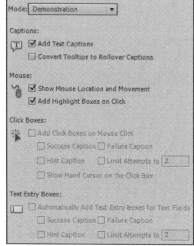

*Default **Demonstration** settings*

*Default **Assessment** settings*

*Default **Training** settings*

Recording Preferences (continued)

Click Boxes

When this option is checked, Captivate converts every click you make during recording into a click box that the student must click during the practice playback.

Text Entry Boxes

When this box is checked, Captivate converts any typing you do into a text entry box that the student must fill in during the practice playback.

Options

Success Caption: Check this box if you want to add a caption after each successful click or text entry to let the students know they were correct.

Failure Caption: By default, Captivate adds captions after each unsuccessful click or text entry to let students know they were incorrect. Uncheck this box if you don't want them.

Hint Caption: Check this if you want to add a rollover caption with a hint that the students see when they roll over the click box or the text entry box.

Limit Attempts to X: By default, students cannot move forward in the practice until they complete the click or typing step correctly. However, you can check this box and indicate the number of attempts allowed before the practice continues automatically.

Show Hand Cursor on the Click Box: Available for click boxes, check this if you want the student's cursor to change to a hand cursor when it is over the click box area. Your students may recognize that this means they are over a hot spot.

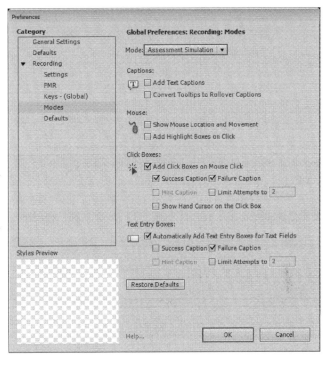

DESIGN TIPS

Here are some important instructional design and usability decisions to make early in your project.

☐ How will you communicate the task your students need to accomplish? Will an audio introduction tell them they are supposed to request a day of vacation in the system?

☐ Do you want to give them step-by-step instructions or just the general task? Will you tell them the first step is to click the **Request Leave** button, or do they need to know that?

☐ If you plan to include step-by-step instructions, where will they appear? Audio? Timed captions? A text box down the side of the slide?

☐ Do you want to show a success caption for each step, or does the fact that the practice continues serve as adequate feedback?

☐ How many attempts should the student get? For a graded assessment, perhaps they should only get one. If the practice is for the student's benefit, perhaps they should have two. Will unlimited attempts cause the user to get frustrated and not be able to finish?

☐ Do you want to provide hints with hint captions and the hand cursor? For a graded assessment, you might not want to. Determine if they add value or not, as the student has to be on the trigger area to see the hints.

☐ How much help do you want to give them in a failure caption? Tell them simply to try again? Remind them what they are supposed to accomplish in general terms? Tell them the specific step? Point to the step?

Recording Preferences (continued)

Defaults Category

Before you record, you can set the styles used for captions, highlight boxes, and other elements to be added to your project.

To change the style, select an option from any of the drop-down menus. Each item has a number of preset styles already available. When you select one, you can see a preview in the **Styles Preview** pane in the bottom corner.

To add your own style, click the **Create New Style** button. New styles are then added to the appropriate drop-down lists. If you have a project open, the style changes apply just to that project. If you don't have a project open, the style changes apply to all future projects as well.

 Styles, p. 98

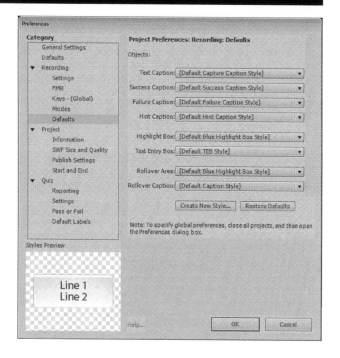

BRIGHT IDEAS

Things to Do DURING Your Capture

Typing

Type carefully. If you fix a typo as you type, the mistake and your correction both show up in the final output. Yes, you can edit it later, but it is quicker to type carefully the first time.

If you are typing something long, such as a sentence or two in a field about why the employee is requesting time off, consider just pasting it in rather than typing it. It can be cumbersome for a student to watch the typing of a long passage, and you are more likely to have a typo in a long passage. Pasting text already typed and ready in another document can be cleaner and easier for everyone.

If you do make a mistake with your typing, press the **Pause** key. Delete all of what you have typed. Press the **Pause** button again, and start typing from the beginning. This separates the bad typing on one slide and starts the new typing on another slide. During editing, delete the slide with the bad typing.

Scrolling and Dragging

Anytime you scroll or drag your mouse, full-motion recording is triggered, unless you have changed the defaults. FMR increases your file size and is hard

to edit, so it is often simpler if you reserve FMR for tasks that really need the moving video. Plan your steps carefully to avoid FMR when it is not needed. For example, if you need to scroll down to the bottom of the screen, click in the bottom of the scroll bar instead of dragging the slider down. If you need to select a word, double-click it instead of highlighting it with the cursor.

Tooltips

As you are capturing your steps, your mouse may be resting on a feature in your software long enough to trigger the tooltip to appear. If it does, it will appear in your capture. Pay attention to these tooltips when they appear, and, if needed, move your mouse and take another screen capture manually to get a good shot.

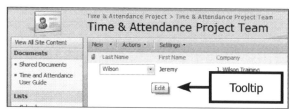

BRIGHT IDEAS

Useful Keyboard Shortcuts

During recording you can use keyboard shortcuts to help you get a good capture. Some of the most useful include:

Pause

Press the **Pause** key on your keyboard if you need to do anything during the capture that you don't want to record. For example:

- A window pops up, and you need to resize it or move it into the recording area.
- You get to a certain step and you realize something isn't set up properly that you need to fix.
- You make a mistake and need to undo it.

While you are paused, the **Captivate** icon in your system tray has a very small orange dot, letting you know you are paused.

When you are done and ready to resume the capture, simply press the **Pause** key again.

Print Screen

During automatic recording, you can manually add an extra screen capture at any time by pressing the **Print Screen** key on your keyboard. Do this any time you aren't sure you got a good capture. For example, perhaps it took an extra second for a dialog box to load, and you aren't sure if the capture took before it fully appeared. It's easier to delete unneeded manual captures than to go back and recreate something you missed.

End

Press the **End** key to finish your capture.

Other Recording Shortcuts

There are a number of other keyboard shortcuts available, and all of them can be customized. You can find them on the **Keys** tab of the **Preferences** dialog box.

 Keys Category, p. 23
Useful Keyboard Shortcuts, p. 224

After Your Capture

You will most likely do a fair amount of editing to your capture once you are done with it. For example, you may add or delete slides and captions, adjust mouse movements, etc. However, it doesn't make sense to spend time fine-tuning your capture this way if there is something wrong with the capture, and it needs to be done over.

When you are finished with your capture, save it, and then walk through each of the slides to check for the following before you start editing:

- ❑ Are there any screens that were still loading when the screen shot was taken?
- ❑ Are there any typos in the on-screen typing?
- ❑ Is there anything showing that the student should not be seeing? A tooltip? An Outlook message indicator? Sensitive data?
- ❑ Are there any steps missing?

These are the big problems that are hard to resolve during editing. It is often quicker to just start the capture over again, rather than trying to fix these problems. Otherwise, you could spend 30-60 minutes trying to fix a problem that could have been eliminated if you took 5 minutes to take the capture over again.

Smaller problems, such as the mouse in the wrong place, are easier to fix during editing. As you become more familiar with taking captures, you'll learn what to look out for and which problems are best resolved with a re-capture.

Editing and Refining Your Captures

In the next several chapters, you'll learn ways to take your raw capture and turn it into a polished lesson or practice.

- Chapters 4 and 6 show you how to add and modify on-screen elements such as text captions and highlight boxes.
- Chapter 5 shows you how to add audio narration.
- Chapter 7 shows you how to add or modify the interactive elements such as an explanatory rollover caption or the click boxes and text entry boxes for a practice.
- Chapter 8 covers a few last features specific to simulations, such as editing mouse movements.

Notes

Adding & Managing Slides

3

Your slides are the backbone of your project. In many cases, when you first create your project, the slides are set up then. For example, if you are creating a software simulation, then each slide is a screen capture, with all of them being played together like a movie in the finished output. If you are importing a PowerPoint presentation, then you'll have one Captivate slide for each of your PowerPoint slides.

In this chapter, you'll learn how to add several slide types that correspond to the project types: blank slides, image slides, and PowerPoint slides. In the next chapter, you'll learn about some additional slide types, such as text animation slides.

You'll also learn how to manage your slides effectively, whether changing the slide properties, creating master slides to create a consistent look, or rearranging and grouping slides to keep them organized.

Slide Type	Chapter
New slide	3
Blank slide	3
PowerPoint slide	3
Question slide	10
Recording slide	8
Image slide	4
Animation slide	4
Master slide	3
Placeholder slide	11

In this chapter:
- New & Blank Slides
- PowerPoint Slides
- Image Slides
- Slide Properties
- Slide Notes
- Master Slides
- Managing Slides

Notes

Insert a New, Blank Slide

To insert a new, blank slide:

1. Go to the **Insert** menu.
2. Select **New Slide** or **Blank Slide**.

With **New Slide**, the added slide uses the master slide of the slide before it. With **Blank Slide**, the added slide is truly blank with no master applied.

 Master Slides, p. 38

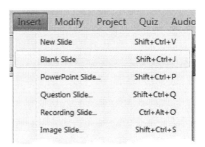

Insert a PowerPoint Slide

To insert individual PowerPoint slides:

1. Go to the **Insert** menu.
2. Select **PowerPoint Slide**.
3. Indicate where you want the slides to appear in your project.
4. Click **OK**.
5. Find and select the file you want.
6. Click **Open**.
7. Enter the properties you want.
8. Click **OK**.

 PowerPoint Import Properties, p. 17

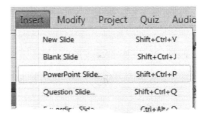

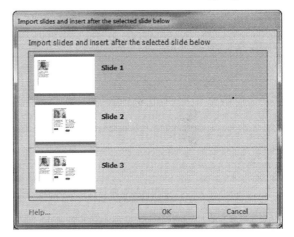

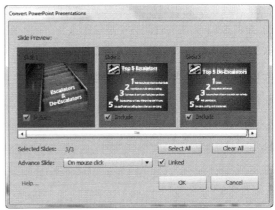

Edit a PowerPoint Slide in Captivate

You can edit a PowerPoint slide right from within Captivate. When you initiate editing, PowerPoint opens up within the Captivate interface, letting you access the capabilities of PowerPoint without having to leave Captivate.

To edit an imported PowerPoint slide from within Captivate:

1. Right-click the slide.
2. Select **Edit with Microsoft PowerPoint**.
3. Select the editing option you want.
4. Make your changes to the slide, using the PowerPoint interface.
5. Click the **Save** button.

Editing Options

Edit Slide: Just the selected slide will be opened for editing.

Edit Presentation: The entire presentation will be opened for editing.

Find Presentation in Library: This highlights the presentation in the **Library**. You can access more editing options from the **Library**.

Export Animation: This option converts the selected slide as an SWF file. You can then save the SWF file and use it in other places such as on a web page or even another Captivate project.

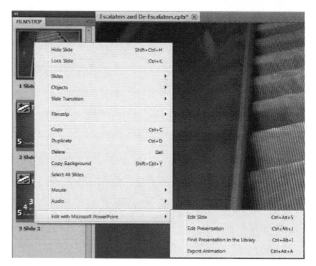

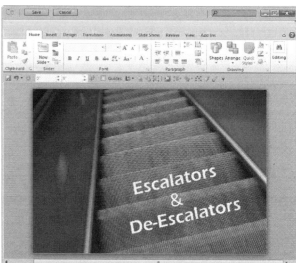

Imported PowerPoint slide being edited in Captivate

Update an Imported Slide

When you have a linked PowerPoint slide, changes made to the PowerPoint source file can be updated in the Captivate file, but it doesn't happen automatically. You need to initiate the update.

To update an imported PowerPoint slide:

1. Right-click the presentation in the **Library**.
2. Select **Update**.
3. Select which embedded presentations you want to update.
4. Click the **Update** button.
5. Click **OK**.

If any new slides have been added to the PowerPoint file, you will be asked to select which ones you want to add.

 Library, p. 184

 BRIGHT IDEAS

- Notice that there are other options on the **Library**'s right-click menu. For example, you can choose to embed the presentation instead of keeping the link active. If you were using an embedded file, there would be an option to change it to a linked file.

- An embedded file also has a **Compact** option. This permanently deletes any slides from the original PowerPoint file that are not currently being used in the Captivate file.

- A green dot next to the presentation in the **Library** tells you that the file is current. The dot becomes orange if it is not current. It becomes a question mark if the link is broken because the file is renamed or moved. Click the question mark to re-establish the link.

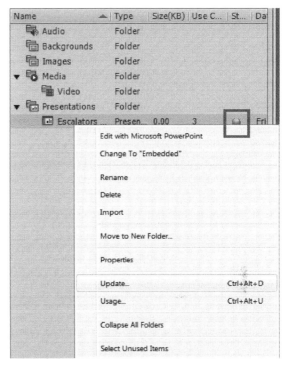

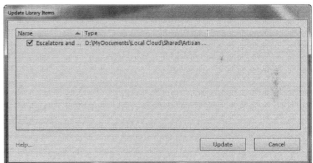

Add an Image Slide

When you add an image slide, the image is merged to the background of the slide. If you want an image to "float" on the slide so that you can time, move, or resize it, add it as an image instead of as an image slide.

Captivate accepts the following image types: .jpg, .gif, .png, .bmp, .ico, .emf, .wmf, .pot, .potx, .pict.

 Add an Image to a Slide, p. 54

To add an image slide:

1. Go to the **Insert** menu.
2. Select **Image Slide**.
3. Find and select the image you want to use.
4. Click **Open**.

The image is now the background of a slide. As such, it can not be repositioned, resized, or edited on the slide.

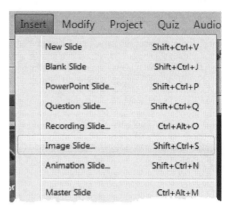

 BRIGHT IDEA

If you want to have the image as part of the background but want to make some changes first (move, resize, rotate, crop, etc.), add it as an image instead of an image slide. Then once you have it how you want it, simply right-click it and merge it to the background.

 Merge With Background, p. 133

You can swap out the image in a background in the **Background** section of the slide properties.

 Slide Properties, p. 35

Accessibility: Click the **Accessibility** button to get a pop-up window that lets you enter a text description for the slide. This text will be read to students using screen readers who cannot see the content of the slide. Either type your text in the space provided, or click the **Import Slide Notes** button to use your slide notes for the accessibility text.

 Accessibility/Section 508, p. 216
Slide Notes, p. 37

Label: You can give a unique name to each slide. This helps during development because the label makes it easier to identify which slide you want to work with. In addition, the slide label is read to students using a screen reader if the accessibility features are turned on for a project.

General Pane

Master Slide: Master slides in Captivate are very much like master slides in PowerPoint. You are able to create slide backgrounds that you can use over and over again. Select the master you want from the drop-down menu.

 Master Slides, p. 38

Stage: If you want to change the background color of the slide, uncheck the **Project Background** box, and then click the **Stage** color swatch to pick a new color or gradient.

 Colors and Color Gradients, p. 90

Background: Every version of the background of every slide is saved in the **Library**. This field shows you what background image is being used. Use the **Browse**, **Delete**, and **Edit** buttons below the field to make changes to the background image. These options are disabled if you are using a master slide or an imported PowerPoint slide.

 Library, p. 184

Quality: This drop-down menu lets you select the image quality of the slide. You can increase the quality to **Optimized**, **JPEG**, or **High (24-bit)** if your published quality is not what you want.

Display Time: By default, each slide shows for three seconds. Adjust the time here or in the **Timeline** panel.

 Timing Objects, p. 105

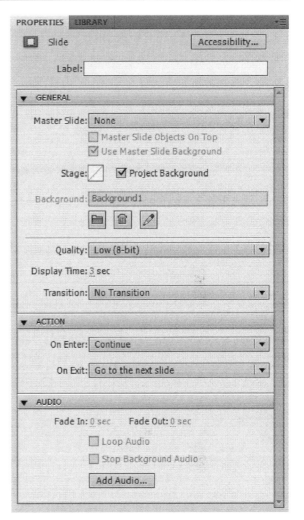

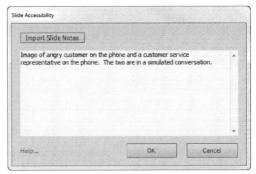

Accessibility text pop-up window

Slide Properties (continued)

General Pane (continued)

Transitions: Transitions are effects that play when a project goes from one slide to the next. A slide transition plays at the beginning of a slide. For example, if a transition is applied to slide 3, it appears when the project goes from slide 2 to slide 3.

 BRIGHT IDEA

You can also apply transitions and effects to individual objects. Apply simple fade in/fade out transitions in the **Transition** pane for that object, or apply special effects such as motion paths or flying in/out from the **Effects** tab.

 Object Transitions, p. 92
Object Effects, p. 102

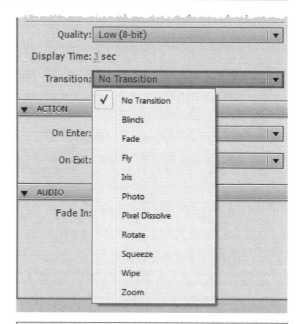

Action Pane

The **Action** pane lets you designate certain actions when the slide first begins (**On Enter**) or when the movie reaches the very last frame of the slide (**On Exit**). For example, you might want to disable a button when the student first comes to a slide.

 CAUTION

An **On Exit** action only runs if the student goes all the way to the end of the slide. If the student leaves before the slide is finished playing (such as clicking a button with a **Go to Next Slide** action), then the **On Exit** action will not play.

 Actions, ch. 7 & 9

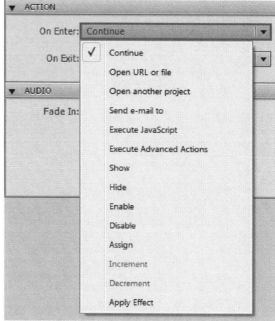

Audio Pane

The **Audio** pane lets you add and manage audio attached to the slide. The options vary slightly based on whether or not there is already audio on the slide.

 Audio, ch. 5

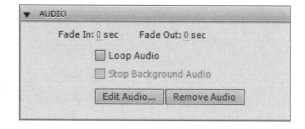

Slide Notes

Slide notes let you put text notes on individual slides. These might be development notes or the transcript of your audio. They are used during development and do not appear in the published movie. When you add your text to the **Slides Notes** panel, you can then:

- View the notes while recording audio.
- Convert the text to computerized audio using the text-to-speech converter.
- Create closed captions for accessibility purposes that <u>do</u> appear in the published movie.

Text-to-Speech, p. 79
Closed Captioning, p. 80
Accessibility/Section 508, p. 216

TIME SAVER

When you import slides from PowerPoint, the slide notes from that file are automatically imported into your Captivate slide notes.

Add Slide Notes

To view the Slide Notes panel:
1. Go to the **Window** menu.
2. Select **Slide Notes**.

To add slide notes:
1. Select the slide you want.
1. Click the **Plus** button in the **Slide Notes** pane.
2. Type or paste your text.
3. Repeat steps 1 and 2 for additional notes for that slide.

To remove slide notes:
1. Select the heading row for the note you want to delete.
2. Click the **Minus** button.

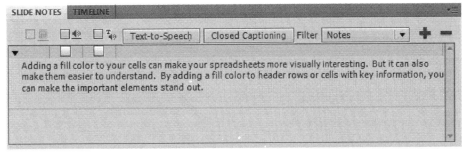

Master Slides

Master slides can help you create a consistent look quickly. Just as with Microsoft PowerPoint, you can add design elements to a master slide that can then be used as the background for one or more of your slides. Master slides are often used for design and branding elements that you want to have appear on more than one slide.

Master slides are managed in the **Master Slide** tab. Go to the **Window** menu, and select **Master Slide** to view the tab. Then masters are applied to individual slides on the Properties panel.

Create a Master Slide

To create a master slide:

1. Go to the **Insert** menu.

2. Select **Master Slide**.

3. With the slide selected in the **Master Slide** tab, configure properties in the **Properties** pane and add elements to the slide in the work area.

Master Slide Properties

Label: Labels are very important for master slides, making it easier to select the one you want for a given slide.

Stage: Click the color picker to select a color for the master slide background, if needed. This option is only available if you uncheck **Project Background**.

Browse: Click the **Browse** button if you want to find and select an image as the slide background. You can select from other backgrounds in the Library or import your own image.

Clear: Click this button to remove the current background image.

Edit: Click this button to edit the image properties of the background image.

Master Slide Objects

Only certain object types can be added to a master slide. Objects that cannot be used are grayed out on the Toolbar and the **Insert** menu.

Timing is not available on slide master objects. The **Timeline** is instead used for visibility, locking, and front-to-back order.

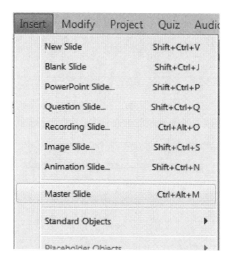

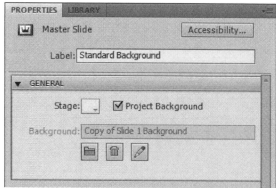

Apply a Master Slide

To apply a master to a project slide:

1. Select the slide(s) you want to apply the master to.
2. In the **Properties** panel, select the master you want from the **Master Slide** menu.

Master Slide Options

Master Slide Objects on Top: By default, the slide master objects appear behind anything you add to the project slide. Check this box if you want the master slide elements to appear on top of the project slide elements. You cannot reorder the order of the individual master objects, but rather they can be moved all to the front or all to the back.

Use Master Slide Background: Keep this checked if you want to use the background image of the slide master. Uncheck this box to enable the rest of the panel, letting you change the background color and image.

 TIME SAVER

Remember that when you insert a *blank* slide, it does not have a slide master. But if you insert a *new* slide, it adopts the master of the slide before it.

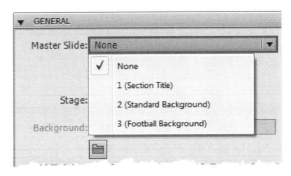

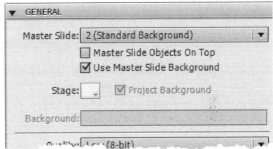

Hide Slides

During the capturing process, it is not uncommon to get unnecessary captures. If you delete these slides and then later realize you need them, you may have a problem. Instead, you can hide the unwanted slides and delete them later when you are sure you don't want them.

Hidden slides do not show up in preview mode or in your published movie.

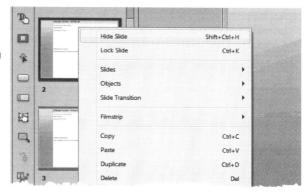

To hide a slide:
1. Right-click the slide thumbnail in the **Filmstrip**.
2. Select **Hide Slide**.

To unhide a slide:
1. Right-click the slide thumbnail.
2. Select **Show Slide**.
 - or -
1. Click the "eyeball" icon under the thumbnail.

Hidden slide

Regular Slide

Delete Slides

To delete a slide:
1. Right-click the slide thumbnail in the **Filmstrip**.
2. Select **Delete**.
 -or-
1. Select the slide in the **Filmstrip**.
2. Press the **Delete** key on your keyboard.

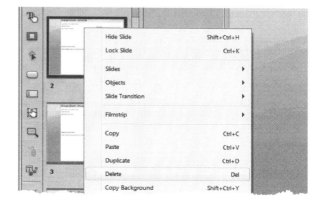

Move Slides

To move a slide to another position in the capture:

1. Click the slide's thumbnail, and drag it to the location you want.

Copy, Paste, and Duplicate Slides

Slides cannot be cut, but they can be copied and pasted. Once you select a slide in the **Filmstrip**, you can copy, paste, and duplicate it four different ways:

- The **Edit** menu **(A)**
- Keyboard shortcuts **(B)**
- The thumbnail right-click menu **(C)**
- The **Main Options** toolbar **(D)**

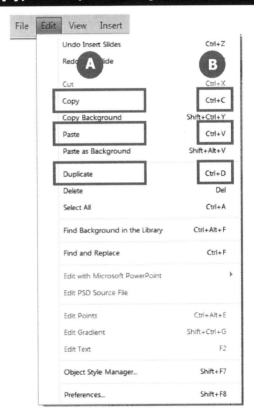

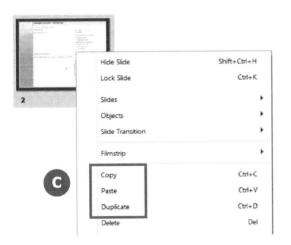

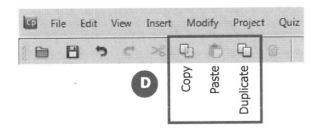

 TIME SAVERS

The duplicate function combines the copy and paste actions into one step. The duplicated slide is pasted directly after the selected slide.

You can select more than one slide when you use these functions. For consecutive slides, press **Shift** while clicking the first and last slide in a range to select the entire range. Press **Ctrl** while clicking slides if they aren't consecutive.

Lock Slides

If you want to ensure that certain slides don't get deleted, you can lock them. Locking a slide also keeps you from adding or editing objects on the slide.

To lock a slide:

1. Right-click the slide thumbnail in the **Filmstrip**.
2. Select **Lock Slide**.

To unlock a slide:

1. Right-click the slide thumbnail.
2. Select **Unlock Slide**.

- or -

1. Click the **Lock** icon in the top corner of the thumbnail.

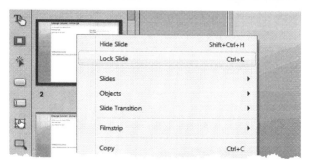

Locked Slide

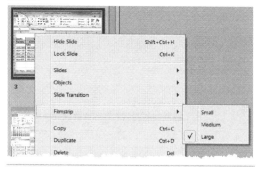

🔆 **BRIGHT IDEA**

You can make the thumbnails in the **Filmstrip** larger or smaller from the thumbnail right-click menu.

Group Slides

Grouping slides can help you manage a large project. When slides are grouped, you can identify them quickly and move, hide, or delete them as a group. Only consecutive slides can be grouped.

To group slides:

1. Select all the slides you want to group together.
2. Right-click any of the selected slides.
3. Select **Group**.
4. Select **Create**.

Once you create a group, the slides are collapsed in the **Filmstrip** with a placeholder slide. When the placeholder is selected, the **Slide Group Properties** pane appears.

Slide Group Properties

Title: When you enter a title in the **Properties** panel, it appears on the placeholder slide and under the thumbnail.

Master Slide: Using this drop-down menu, you can change the master slide for all of the slides in the group at once.

 Master Slides, p. 38

Color: Use the color picker to set the outline color used in the **Filmstrip**. Using different colors can make it easy to find the slides you are looking for.

Managing Groups

To expand a group:

1. Click the down arrow icon on the group placeholder thumbnail. **(A)**

To collapse a group:

1. Click the up arrow icon on the thumbnail of the first slide in the group. **(B)**

To ungroup slides:

1. Right-click any of the slides in the group.
2. Select **Group**.
3. Select **Remove**.

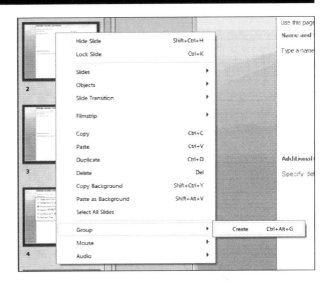
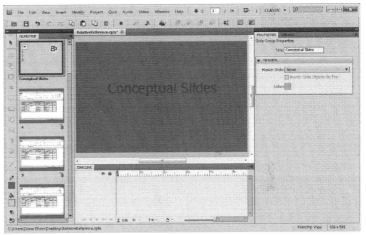

Collapsed Group

Expanded Group

Notes

Adding Content Objects

4

The next several chapters deal with how to add content to your slides.

- In this chapter, you'll learn about adding content objects, including captions, images, shapes, highlight boxes, and animations.
- Chapter 5 covers how to add audio and video to your projects.
- Chapter 6 covers object properties that relate to most object types, such as how to select colors, how to apply styles, and how to adjust timing.
- In chapter 7, you'll learn how to add interactive objects such as rollover objects, text entry boxes, and buttons.
- In chapter 10, you'll learn how to add questions and quizzes.

In this chapter:
- Captions
- Images
- Shapes & Highlight Boxes
- Animations
- Text Animations
- Zoom Areas

Notes

Working With Captions

Captions are one way to add text to your slides, whether you want to point out a step in a computer procedure, provide feedback on a practice activity, provide instructions on what to do, or add text in a branching scenario.

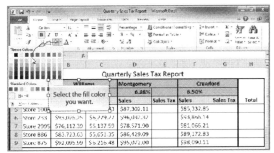

Reinforce teaching points

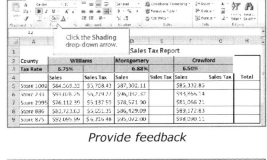

Provide feedback

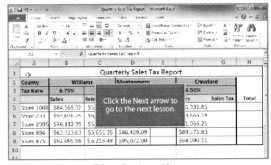

Give instructions

Add "non-caption" text

 DESIGN TIP

You can also add text to shapes. Shapes don't have all of the behind-the-scenes logic that captions have (like automatic recording or exporting), but you have more formatting options, such as custom colors and gradients.

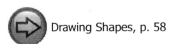 Drawing Shapes, p. 58

Add a New Caption

To add a new caption:

1. Click the **Insert Caption** button.

2. Type your caption text.

3. Configure any settings in the caption **Properties** panel.

4. Click off the caption.

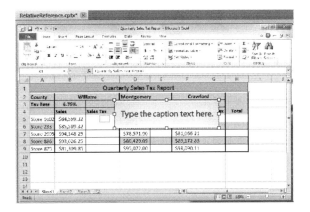

Generating Automatic Captions

When you take screen captures, you can choose to have Captivate automatically add captions for every click. This can save a tremendous amount of time in your development process.

Configure Automatic Captioning

To set up automatic captioning:

1. Go to the **File** menu.
2. Select **Preferences**.
3. Select the **Modes** category.
4. Click the **Mode** drop-down menu.
5. Select the mode you want to configure.
6. Check the **Add Text Captions** box to turn on automatic captioning.
7. Click the **OK** button.

You can also get to the **Preferences** dialog box by clicking the Settings button in the recording window.

 Recording Preferences, p. 24

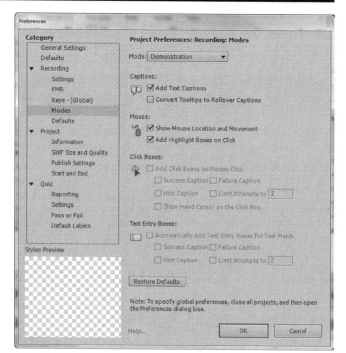

 CAUTION

Automatic captioning may not work on every software application. The names of your software elements (buttons, menus, etc.) must be set up in a way that Captivate can recognize. Otherwise, you'll need to manually add and/or edit the captions.

DESIGN TIPS

- Create a style guide for your procedural terminology so that your language is consistent. For example:

  Do you refer to a drop-down or a drop-down arrow?

  Do you bold the name of the feature or put it in quotations?

  Do you always capitalize the name of a feature, never capitalize it, or match what is in the system?

  Web Resource:
  Style Guide Template

- You may end up resizing your finished movie down to a smaller size to fit on a web page or in a course interface. If you are likely to do this, make your captions a larger font size than you think you need. That way they are still legible when you shrink the movie.

- Never sacrifice legibility for creativity! Consider the color scheme of the software being captured, the color and size of the caption and the color and size of the text to make sure the captions stand out and are easy to read.

Legible

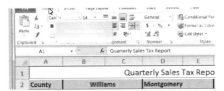
Not legible

POWER TIP

You may use different terminology and punctuation than the automatic captions do. Rather than edit each caption, you can change the template used for the captions.

 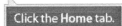
Original format   *Your preference*

First, you need to find the text template document for the language you want, which is in your program files. Make a backup copy of it in case you want to return to the original template. Then open the file in Notepad or Wordpad to edit it.

As you scroll through the document, it may seem overwhelming, but it is really quite simple. If you look at the end of every line, you'll see there is one group for each type of software feature (button, tab, etc.). Within each group, you can see the language to be used in the caption, shown in quotation marks. **%s** indicates the name of the software feature, such as **Home**, as in the example above.

Make whatever changes you want to the text INSIDE the quotation marks at the end of each line, being very careful not to change anything else or delete the **%s**.

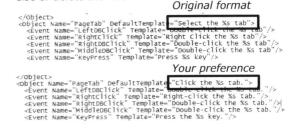

Then, save the file. You can then share this file with anyone else on your development team. They just need to copy the file over the one currently in their program files.

Edit Caption Text

To make text edits to your captions:

1. Double-click the caption to get a cursor.
2. Make your edits.
3. Click off the caption.

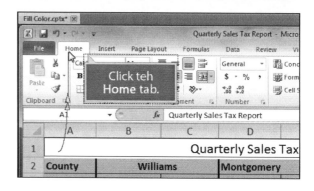

Formatting Caption Text

Formatting is done in the **Properties** panel. Select the text you want to format, or click on the caption if you want to format all the text in the caption.

Character Pane

Family: Select the font type you want.

Style: Select the font style you want.

Size: Type or drag your mouse for the point size you want.

Format: Click the buttons for bold, italics, and underlining, superscript, or subscript, as needed.

Color: Click the swatch to select the font color.

Highlight: Click the swatch to select the color for highlighting the text.

 Colors, p. 90

Format Pane

Align: Select the button you want for horizontal and vertical alignment of text within the caption.

Indentation: Click the **Decrease Indent** or **Increase Indent** buttons to change the left margin on the caption.

Numbering: Select a numbering option from the drop-down menu to add bullets or different styles of numbering, as needed.

Line Spacing: Type or drag your mouse to change the vertical spacing between lines.

Insert: click the **Insert Symbol** button to insert symbols such as a copyright symbol or a foreign currency symbol.

POWER TIP

You can insert variables into a caption. For example, you might want a caption that displays the current date, the score of a test, the answer to a question, etc.

 Variables, p. 139

Change Caption and Callout Type

The caption type determines the color, shape, and outline of the captions. The callout type determines if and where the caption is pointing.

To change the caption type:

1. Select the caption you want to change.
2. In the **General** pane, click the **Caption type** drop-down menu.
3. Select the caption type you want.

To change the callout type:

1. Select the caption you want to change.
2. In the **General** pane, click the **Callout Type** drop-down menu.
3. Select the callout type you want.

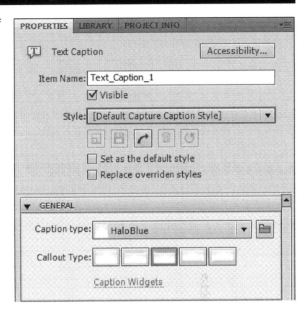

 BRIGHT IDEA

You an also insert caption widgets, giving you more choices for your caption type. In the **General** pane of the caption's properties, click the **Caption Widgets** link to open the **Widgets** pane. From there, click the **Insert** link for the one you want.

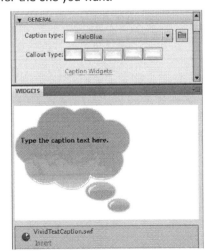

 Widgets, p. 186

DESIGN TIPS

- Use different caption types for different purposes. For example, you could use Adobe Blue when the student should read and Glass Blue when the student should act.

- Use a transparent caption when you want to put plain text on a slide. For example, you might want to fill in a blank on a form or add a title to the top of a slide.

- Remember, you can use styles to save and apply formatting attributes.

 Styles, p. 98

 CAUTION

If you change the caption type, it may also change your font settings for that caption. So be sure to select the type you want before you format the text.

Caption and Text Formatting Options

Font Style Menu Options
Options vary based on the font chosen.

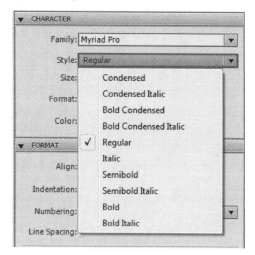

Typical Callout Types
Options vary based on the caption type chosen.

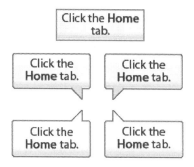

Numbering Menu Options

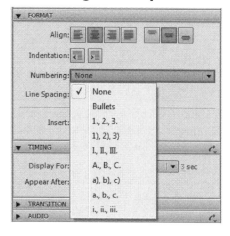

Caption Types

 Web Resource:
Caption Type Reference Guide

 POWER TIP

If none of the existing caption types fit your needs perfectly, you can create your own using photo editing software. Search Captivate help for **custom text caption files** to get the details.

Exporting and Importing Captions

Exporting caption text can be useful for creating print materials such as a job aid. You can also export captions, make changes to them, and import them back into your project—a huge time saver when you have lots of edits or if you need to translate/localize the captions.

Adobe Captivate				Wednesday, October 20, 2010
Slide Id	Item Id	Original Text Caption Data	Updated Text Caption Data	Slide
961	975	Select **Quarterly Sales Tax Report**	Select the cell(s) you want to format.	3
997	1011	Select **Shading**	Click the **Shading** drop-down arrow.	6
1017	1031	Select the **No Fill** menu item	Select the fill color you want.	7

Caption as exported   Edited caption to import

Export Captions

To export captions

1. Go to the **File** menu.
2. Select **Export**.
3. Select **Project Captions and Closed Captions**.
4. Find and select the folder where you want to save the Word document.
5. Click the **Save** button.

TIME SAVER

If you plan to use the exported captions in other documents, such as a help manual, set up a macro in Word to delete the unneeded columns and rows and take the text out of the table. Then, with one stroke, you have a ready-to-use list of steps.

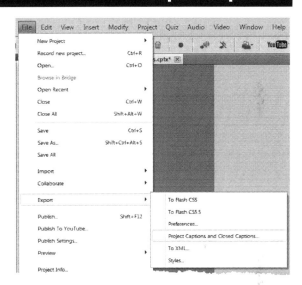

Import Captions

To import captions

1. Go to the **File** menu.
2. Select **Import**.
3. Select **Project Captions and Closed Captions**.
4. Find and select the document previously exported.
5. Click the **Open** button.

CAUTION

For the import to work properly, make sure you import back into the same Captivate file. Avoid adding, deleting, or rearranging slides between import and export. And be sure to only change the caption text in the Word document and not add/delete rows, change Item Id numbers, etc.

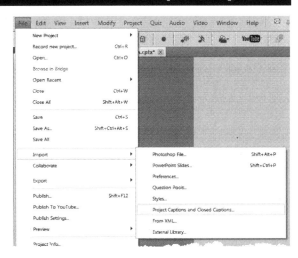

Add an Image to a Slide

To add an image to a slide:

1. Go to the **Insert** menu.
2. Select **Image**.
3. Find and select the image you want to use.
4. Click **Open**.

The image is now an object on the slide which can be moved, resized, deleted, timed to audio, etc.

 TIME SAVER

You can also add an image by:

- Pasting it. For example, you can copy an image from a PowerPoint document or a Photoshop file and paste it onto a slide.
- Dragging and dropping it. Open up the folder with the image, and drag the image onto the slide.

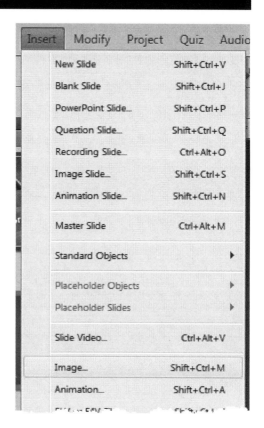

Image Properties

Many of the properties and options for an image are the same as for any other object type, such as moving, resizing, and timing an image. Learn more about these settings in chapter 6. In this section, you will learn about some of the properties and options unique to an image.

Image Pane

Make the Selected Color Transparent: You can select a single color and make it transparent in your image. This is useful for removing the white background in a photo or clipart.

To make a color transparent:

1. Click the color swatch in the top pane of the **Properties** panel.

2. Click the eyedropper icon.

3. Click the color in the image that you want to make transparent.

Reset to Original Size: If you have resized the image, click this button to return it to its original size. This option does not undo cropping.

Image Edit Pane

Brightness: Move the slider right or enter a positive number to brighten the image. Move the slider to the left or enter a negative number to darken the image.

Sharpness: Move the slider right or enter a positive number to better define the edges in the image. Move the slider to the left or enter a negative number to soften the edges.

Contrast: Move the slider right or enter a positive number to increase the contrast (make darks darker, lights lighter and colors brighter). Move the slider to the left or enter a negative number to reduce the contrast.

Alpha: Alpha refers to the opacity of an image. 100% means fully opaque. Use a lower number if you want to make the image partially or fully transparent.

Hue: Move the slider left or right to change the colors of the image. For example, sliding it one way might make an image more blue and sliding it the other way might make it more red.

Saturation: Move the slider right or enter a positive number to increase the saturation (richness) of the colors. Move the slider to the left or enter a negative number to make them less saturated.

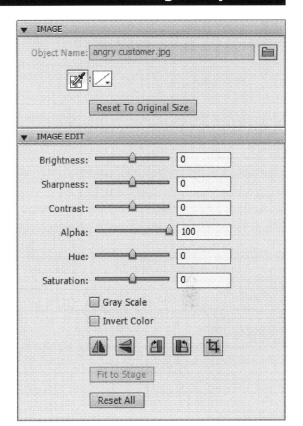

Image Properties (continued)

Gray Scale: Check this box to remove all color in the image and convert it to gray scale.

Invert Color: Check this box to change darks to lights, lights to darks, and all colors to their opposite on the color wheel. This gives the appearance of a film negative.

Rotation Icons: Click any of the four rotation options to flip or rotate the image.

 Transform Pane, p. 93

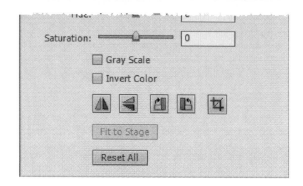

Crop: Click the **Crop** button to bring up the **Resize Image/Crop** dialog box.

Drag the crop frame handles and move the crop frame to indicate the part of the image you want to keep. That portion of the image will then appear as large as possible on the slide.

Constrain Proportions: If you are cropping the image, check this box to make the crop frame the same aspect ratio as the slide. Uncheck it if you want to be able to change the aspect ratio.

Fit to Stage: This option enlarges or shrinks the image to the largest size that will fit fully on the slide. Because the aspect ratio (height/width proportion) may be different on the image than on the slide, you may end up with empty space either above and below or to the left and right of the image.

Reset All: Click this button to return the image to its original settings. However, this does not undo any cropping.

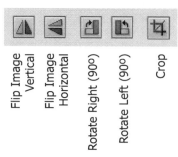

Flip Image Vertical — Flip Image Horizontal — Rotate Right (90°) — Rotate Left (90°) — Crop

 CAUTION

If you crop out areas of your image, you cannot come back later and bring those areas back. If you wanted those parts of the image back, you would either need to re-add the image or find the uncropped version in the **Library** and add it back.

 Library, p. 184

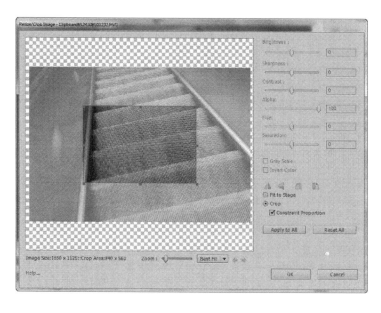

Using Photoshop Files

In addition to using image types such as GIF and PNG, you can import Photoshop PSD files. When you do, you can bring in each layer individually for more control, edit the file in Photoshop without leaving Captivate, and update the image when the source file changes.

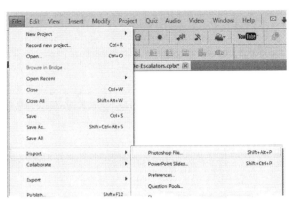

To import a Photoshop file:

1. Go to the **File** menu.
2. Select **Import**.
3. Select **Photoshop File**.
4. Find and select the file you want
5. Click the **Open** button.
6. Select the options you want.
7. Click **OK**.

Photoshop Import Options

Photoshop Layer Comps: In Photoshop, you can create several versions of a design in the same file. These versions are called layer comps. If you have more than one comp in your file, select **Multiple**, and then select the comp you want from the drop-down menu.

Scale According to Stage Size: If you check this box, Captivate will resize the image to be a large as possible and still fit on the slide.

Select Photoshop Layers to Import: If your Photoshop file has layers, check or uncheck the box for each layer to indicate which ones you want to import. Each layer will appear as its own image in Captivate.

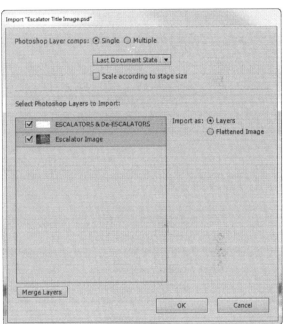

Import As: If your Photoshop file has layers, but you want to import it all as a single image, select **Flattened Image**. This will bring it in as a single image without changing the layers of the underlying Photoshop file.

Merge Layers: If you don't want the image flattened but do want some of the layers combined, select the layers you want to merge (shift-click the layer names), and then click the **Merge Layers** button.

To edit a Photoshop file from Captivate:

1. Right-click the image (layer) in the **Library**.
2. Select **Edit with**.
3. Find and select Photoshop in your system files.
4. Click the **Open** button.
5. Make your changes in Photoshop.
6. Save your changes.

(Steps 3 and 4 are only necessary the first time you edit an image this way.)

 **POWER TIP**

If you have the Adobe eLearning Suite installed, your imported PSD is linked to the underlying source file. Just as with a linked PowerPoint slide, a green dot next to the file in the **Library** means you are working with the most updated version. A red dot means there has been a change to the source file. A question mark means the link has been broken. Click the red dot or question mark to update or relink the file.

Drawing Shapes

The drawing tools in Captivate let you create your own shapes and lines. For example, you might want to create a simple diagram, add a colored box behind some text, etc.

Your options include line, rectangle, oval, and polygon. Refer to chapter 6 for information on shape properties, such as fill and stroke colors.

Add a Shape or Line

To add a shape or line:

1. Click and hold the shape tool.

2. Select the shape tool you want.

3. Drag your mouse to create the shape you want (for lines, rectangles, and ovals) or click in the work area for each point you want to create (for a polygon).

 DESIGN TIPS

- For a perfect square or circle, press and hold the **Shift** key while drawing a rectangle or oval.

- When drawing a line or polygon, press and hold the **Shift** key while drawing to keep the lines at 45º increments.

- To change the points on a polygon (such as the arrow), right-click the shape, and select **Edit Points.**

- To add text to a shape, double-click the shape, or right-click the shape, and select **Add Text**.

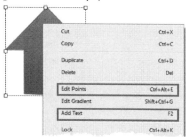

- To use the same drawing tool several times, hold the **Ctrl** key when you click the tool, which lets you use that drawing tool until you press **Escape** or another tool.

- To give a rectangle rounded corners, go to the **Properties** panel and change the value for **Corner radius**.

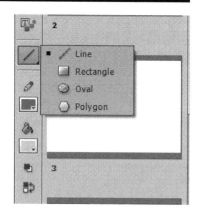

Line tool:
Click and drag

Rectangle tool:
Click and drag

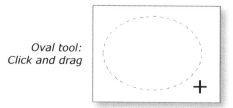

Oval tool:
Click and drag

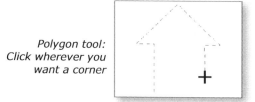

Polygon tool:
Click wherever you want a corner

Add a Highlight Box

A highlight box is a different way to add a rectangle. They are commonly used to add visual emphasis to parts of the screen being discussed.

To add a highlight box:

1. Click the **Insert Highlight Box** tool.

2. Move and resize the highlight box over the area you want to highlight.

3. Format the highlight box in the **Properties** panel.

Options: Fill Outer Area

By default, the highlight box is filled with your fill color on the inside. If you check this option, the inside of the box remains clear, and the outside of the box is filled, creating a more noticeable spotlight effect.

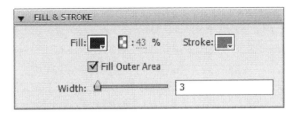

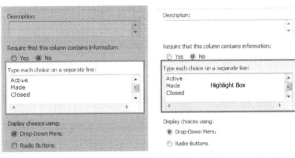

Default inner fill   *Fill Outer Area selected*

DESIGN TIP

How do you decide if you want a rectangle or a highlight box?

Rectangles:

- Have more formatting options, such as gradients and rounded corners.

- Can contain text.

- Can have accessibility text.

- Can have the points edited.

Highlight boxes:

- Can have styles, making it quicker to get the formatting you want.

- Can have an inner fill or an outer fill.

- Can be added automatically to highlight the object you are clicking during a screen capture session.

- Can be used to export the part of the background behind the highlight box, making a quick job aid with just the button, menu, etc. being clicked for each step.

Styles, p. 98
Recording Settings, p. 24
Publish to Print, p. 212

CAUTION

Don't worry if your fill box is missing. Highlight boxes with an outer area fill do not show the fill in the work area. You can only see the fill when previewing or viewing the published movie.

Adding Animations

Animations are a great way to add specialized interactions, functionality, or visual effects. Animations might come from Adobe Flash, game or interaction software that outputs to Flash, an animated GIF that you create in Photoshop or purchase from stock clipart sources, or it might even be a published Captivate project.

When you add an animation slide, the animation becomes part of the background of the slide. This means that the animation cannot be resized, repositioned, or adjusted in the Timeline. When you add an animation to an existing slide, it becomes an object on that slide that can be edited, moved, etc.

 DESIGN TIP

Captivate comes with a gallery of Flash animations you can use in your projects. Look for the **Gallery** folder in your Adobe Captivate system files.

Add an Animation Slide

To add an animation slide:

1. Go to the **Insert** menu.
2. Select **Animation Slide**.
3. Find and select the animation you want.
4. Click the **Open** button.

 CAUTION

- Make sure the frame rate of any inserted animations is the same frame rate as your project. Otherwise, you may get some unpredictable results. The default setting for Captivate projects is 30 frames per second, which can be changed in **Preferences** on the **Edit** menu.

- If you are creating a Flash file for use in Captivate, use embedded fonts instead of system fonts. Otherwise, your text may not appear properly.

 BRIGHT IDEA

Even though the animation on an animation slide does not appear as its own object, you can still change it or delete it. In the **Properties** panel for the slide, click the **Browse** button to select a different animation or the **Clear** button to delete the animation from the slide.

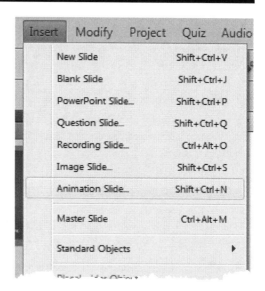

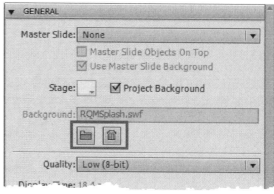

Add an Animation

To add an animation:

1. Go to the **Insert** menu.
2. Select **Animation**.
3. Find and select the animation you want.
4. Click the **Open** button.

Animation Properties Pane

Animations placed as objects on slides have an extra section in the **Properties** panel for animation properties.

Object Name:

Information: Click the information icon next to the **Object Name** to see the Flash version, size, duration, and other information about the animation. (Information provided varies based on the type of animation being used.)

If you are using Captivate as part of the Adobe eLearning Suite, you have the following options available:

Linkage: This shows the link to the file.

Update: Click this button to update the published animation if the linked file has changed.

Source: If your animation was created in Flash, you can link to the corresponding FLA file, making it quicker to edit the animation in Flash.

Edit: If the FLA file is shown in the Source field, you can click the **Edit** button to edit the FLA file.

Alpha: Reduce the percentage if you want the animation to become partially or fully transparent.

Swap: Click this button to replace the animation with another animation, either from the **Library** or via import.

Timing Properties Pane

In addition to the standard options of **Display for** and **Appear After**, there are two additional options available for animations.

Synchronize with Project: Check this box to help synchronize your animation with the **Timeline** speed. It is helpful to try checking this box if your animation is not playing smoothly.

Loop: Check this box if you want the animation to continue back at the beginning when it is finished, until the slide itself is done playing.

 Timing Slide Objects, p. 105

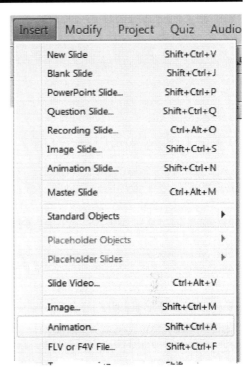

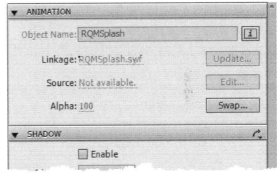

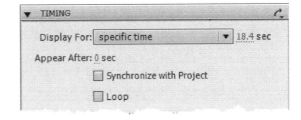

Add a Text Animation

Captivate comes with a wizard that lets you quickly create your own text-based animations.

To create a text animation:

1. Click the **Insert Text Animation** tool.
2. Enter your text in the **Text** field of the dialog box.
3. Format your text.
4. Click the **OK** button.
5. In the **Properties** panel, select the animation effect you want from the **Effect** menu. **(A)**

To make text and font formatting changes later:

1. Click the **Properties** button in the **Properties** panel. **(B)**
2. Make your changes in the dialog box.
3. Click **OK**.

DESIGN TIPS

- Make each individual letter appear faster or slower by changing the value in the **Delay** field. This is the number of seconds between each letter.

- Check the **Loop** box if you want the animation to play over and over until the end of the object's time in the **Timeline**.

Web Resource:
Text Animation Options

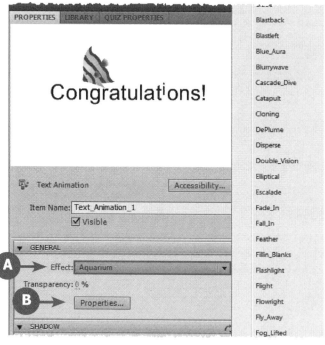

Zoom Areas

Zoom areas take a portion of your slide and magnify it for the student. For example, if you are doing a screen recording and want to emphasize a certain set of tools on screen, you can use a zoom area to magnify that section of the screen.

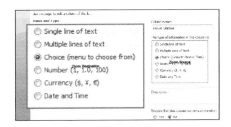

Insert a Zoom Area

To add a zoom area:

1. Click the **Insert Zoom Area** tool.

2. Move and resize the **Zoom Source** box over the area you want to magnify.

3. Move and resize the **Zoom Destination** box to the position and magnification you want for the magnification.

Objects as they first appear on the slide

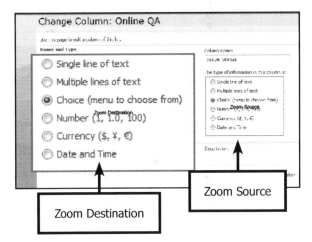

Zoom Source

Zoom Destination

 BRIGHT IDEA

As with most objects, you can use the **Timeline** to indicate when the zoom area will appear and disappear. In addition, you can control how fast or slow it zooms in, by clicking and dragging the divider line in the object placeholder. Drag it to the left for a faster zoom or to the right for a slower zoom.

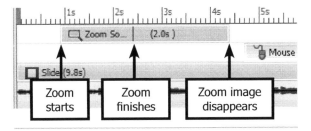

Zoom starts

Zoom finishes

Zoom image disappears

Notes

Audio & Video 5

Audio can be used to add voiceover narration, add fun or dramatic effects with sounds, or set a certain tone or mood with music. In Captivate, you can add audio files to individual objects, individual slides, or the project as a whole.

Audio can be either imported or recorded directly in audio. If you are recording screen captures, you can either record in Captivate while you capture or add it after the capture is finished. MP3 and WAV files can be imported into Captivate.

Captivate also provides useful audio tools such as text-to-speech, which adds automated narration based on the text you enter, as well as closed captions for those who are unable to hear your audio (for technical, environmental, or physical reasons).

In chapter 6, you'll learn how to time individual elements to audio, so that the right text, image, or other object appears exactly when it should.

In addition to audio, you can add video files to your projects. For example, you might want to introduce a course on a new policy with a short video introduction from the CEO.

Notes

Import Audio to the Background

Background audio plays across slides—in the background! Even if you have background audio, you can still have slide-level audio, such as narration. For example, if you want background music in your project, this is how to add it.

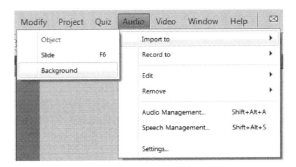

To import audio to the background:

1. Click the **Audio** menu.
2. Select **Import to**.
3. Click **Background**.
4. Navigate to and select the file you want.
5. Click **Open**.
6. Set the background audio options you want.
7. Click the **Save** button.
8. Click the **Close** button.

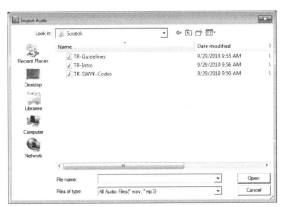

Background Audio Options

Fade In/Fade Out: If you want the background audio to fade in or out, enter the duration of each fade, in seconds.

Loop Audio: By default, this box is checked, meaning the audio will play over and over until the movie is over. Uncheck it if you want the audio to play only once.

Stop Audio at End of Project: By default, this box is checked, meaning that when the movie is over, the audio will stop. Uncheck it if you want the audio to continue playing until the window is closed.

Adjust Background Audio Volume on Slides With Audio: By default, background audio will lower to 50% volume on any slide with its own audio (such as voiceover narration). Uncheck this box if you don't want the audio automatically reduced, or use the slider to change how much to reduce the volume.

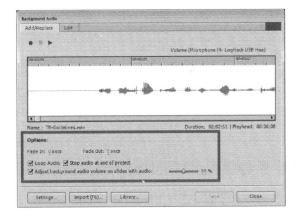

DESIGN TIP

Just because you can doesn't mean you should! Use background audio with care as it can easily overpower or distract from your instructional goals.

TIME SAVER

Captivate comes with music and sound effects in the Gallery!

> ▸ Computer (C:) ▸ Program Files (x86) ▸ Adobe ▸ Adobe Captivate 5.5 ▸ Gallery ▸ Sound

Import Audio to an Object

You can add audio to individual objects such as a specific caption. For example, you can add a cheering sound effect to the correct feedback caption in a practice activity.

1. Select the object you want to import the audio to.
2. Click the **Audio** menu.
3. Select **Import to**.
4. Click **Object**.
5. Navigate to and select the file you want.
6. Click **Open**.
7. Click **Yes** to extend the caption length, if needed.
8. Click **Close**.

 ## CAUTION

You can still adjust the length of the object in the **Timeline**. However, if you make the object shorter than the audio, the audio will get cut off.

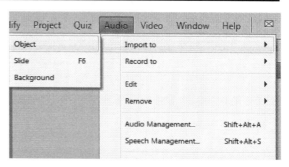

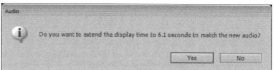

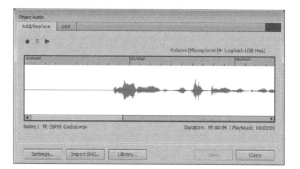

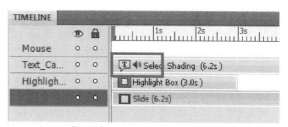

An audio indicator appears on the object in the Timeline.

Import Audio to One or More Slides

To import audio to one or more slides:

1. Select the slide you want to import audio to, or select the first slide if the audio is for the whole movie.
2. Click the **Audio** menu.
3. Select **Import to**. **(A)**
4. Click **Slide**.
5. Navigate to and select the file you want.
6. Click **Open**. **(B)**
7. Choose how to import the audio. **(C)**
8. Click **OK**.

Import Options

The dialog box in step 7 only appears if the imported audio is longer than the slide you are importing it into. The three options determine how that audio is distributed.

Show the slide for the same amount of time as the length of the audio file

Use this option if you are importing audio for a single slide and you want to make the slide as long as the audio.

Distribute the audio file over several slides

Use this if you are importing audio for more than one slide, such as the whole movie. This brings up dialog box that lets you slice up the audio across the slides.

Retain current slide duration and distribute the audio files over several slides

Use this if you are importing audio for more than one slide, but you want Captivate to split up the audio, based on the current slide lengths.

DESIGN TIP

Which option is best? Generally, when you record voiceover for computer simulations, it is best to record the entire script in one file. This tends to take less time and create a more natural tone and flow than trying to record each slide's audio as a separate file. Then, all you need to do is add the one audio file to the first slide and select the middle import option, which lets you chop up the audio across the slides.

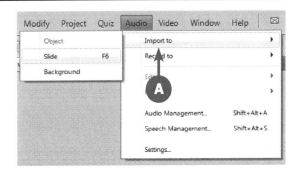

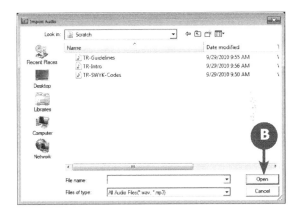

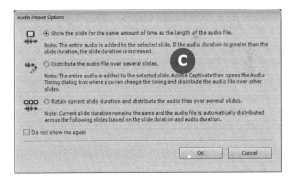

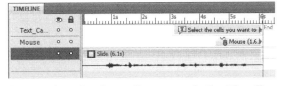

*The waveform for the audio appears in the **Timeline**.*

Distribute Audio Across Slides

When you record your audio in a single file, you then need to distribute it across the slides. If you select the **Distribute the audio...** option when importing, the dialog box appears automatically. Otherwise, you can go to the **Audio** menu to bring up the dialog box.

1. Click the **Audio** menu.
2. Select **Edit**.
3. Select **Project**.
4. Click **Yes** in the warning dialog box (if appropriate).
5. Click the **Play** button to play the audio.
6. Click the **Start Next Slide** button when you get to the point where you want the next slide to start.

   - or -

6. Click in the waveform where you want the next slide to start.
7. Click the **Start Next Slide** button.
8. Click and drag slide dividers to adjust the position.
9. Click the **Save** button.
10. Click the **Close** button.

 Web Resource: Audio Timing Screencast

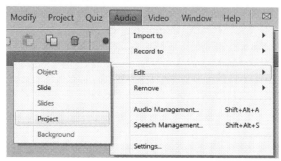

CAUTION

Pay attention to the warning in step 4. If you have closed captions already timed to audio, continuing with this process will remove the timing. Therefore, it is best to time your closed captions at the end of production. After that, use only the slide-level audio editing options.

> If you edit the project audio, all closed captions in the project will be disabled and the timing information of the captions will be lost. However, after editing the audio, you can:
>
> * Enable the closed captions by selecting the Audio CC check boxes in the Slide Notes panel.
>
> * Adjust the timing of the captions by clicking the Closed Captioning tab in the Slide Audio dialog box (Audio > Edit > Slide).
>
> Do you want to continue?

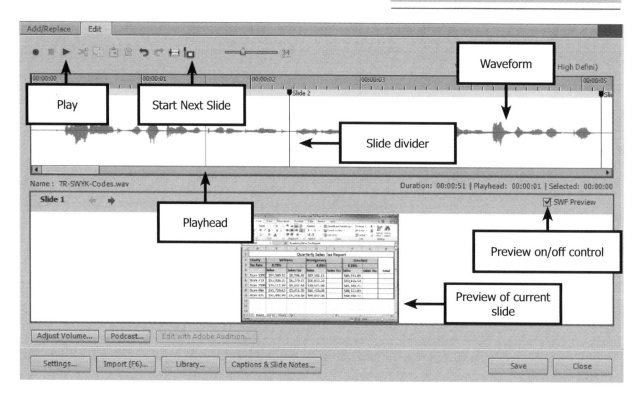

Configure Audio Compression

The audio settings apply to the entire published file, whether you import the audio or record it in Captivate.

1. Click the **Audio** menu.
2. Select **Settings**.
3. Select the compression level you want in the **Bitrate** section.
4. Click **OK**.

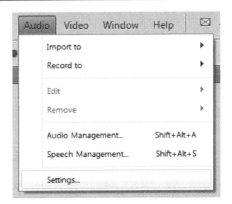

 BRIGHT IDEA

What is bitrate?

The bitrate determines how many points along the sound wave curve are captured in a digital file. It is measured in kbps (kilobits per second).

The more points captured, the higher the quality and the higher the file size.

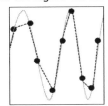 

| Lower bitrate | Higher bitrate |

Constant Bitrate captures the same number of points for the entire project. **Variable Bitrate** adjusts the number of points based on what is happening in the audio. For example, variable bitrate uses fewer points during pauses than during spoken words. For voiceover, variable bitrate is likely to give you the same quality as constant bitrate, but at a lower file size.

If you use constant bitrate, the 48 to 96 range offers a good balance between compression and quality.

When you record audio directly in Captivate, it records at a high quality. The settings you make here determine how it is compressed when you publish. This way, you aren't locked into a certain quality.

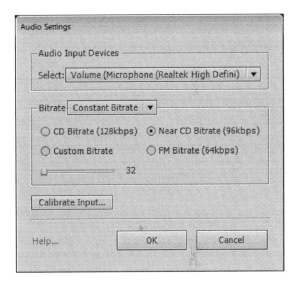

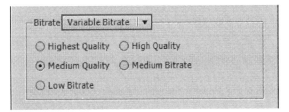

 **CAUTION**

Make sure you test the audio settings by publishing your file and testing it on a target computer. A small change in bitrate can significantly affect quality and file size, so make sure you have the right balance.

Calibrate Audio Input

Before recording audio in Captivate, you will want to calibrate your microphone for the best volume levels. You will be prompted to do it the first time you record audio per session (once for every time you launch Captivate), or you can do it yourself at any time using the procedure below.

To calibrate audio input:

1. Click the **Audio** menu.
2. Select **Settings**.
3. Select the microphone you want to use (if you have more than one available).
4. Click the **Calibrate Input** button.
5. Click the **Auto calibrate** button.
6. Speak into the microphone until you see the **Input Level OK** message.
7. Click **OK**.

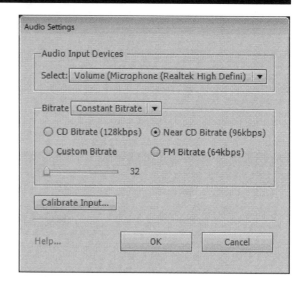

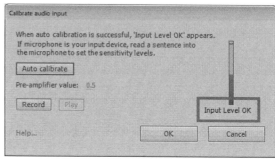

POWER TIP

You can manually control the calibration. Instead of clicking **Auto calibrate**, click the **Record** button, and record some audio. Click the **Stop** button, and then the **Play** button to listen to it.

From there, you can adjust the pre-amplifier value to get the volume you want during recording.

- 1 means no change in audio.
- Less than 1 means the recording volume will be reduced.
- Higher than 1 (up to 10) means the recording volume will be increased.

BRIGHT IDEA

You will want to calibrate your audio every time you sit down to record audio. However, if you are recording more than one project in a sitting, you don't need to recalibrate for each file you work on.

Record Audio to a Slide or Object

To record audio to a slide or project:

1. Select the slide or object you want to record audio to.
2. Click the **Audio** menu.
3. Select **Record to.**
4. Select **Slide** or **Object**.
5. Click the **Record** button.
6. Speak into your microphone.
7. Click the **Stop** button.
8. Click the **Save** button.
9. Click the **Close** button.

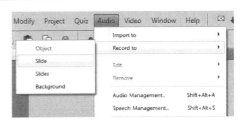

BRIGHT IDEA

If you've added your script in the **Slide Notes** panel, click the **Captions & Slide Notes** button to refer to them while you record.

Record Audio Across Slides

To record audio across several slides:

1. Click the **Audio** menu.
2. Select **Record to.**
3. Select **Slides**.
4. Indicate the range of slides you want to record.
5. Click the **OK** button.
6. Click the **Record** button.
7. Speak into your microphone for the first slide.
8. Click the **Stop** button.
9. Click the **Next Slide** button.
10. Repeat steps 7-9 until all the slides are done.
11. Click the **Save** button.
12. Click the **Close** button.

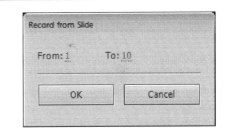

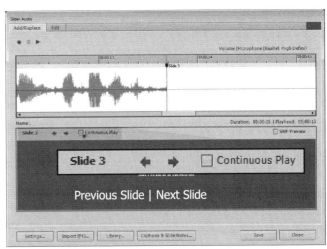

BRIGHT IDEA

If your slides are already set to the exact length you want, you can click the **Continuous Play** checkbox to have the slides auto-advance for you, based on their current timings.

Record Audio While Capturing

If you want to record your narration while doing your initial capture, you can set that up in your initial recording settings. Simply select the microphone you want to use from the **Audio** drop-down menu. Then, speak into your microphone while you are capturing.

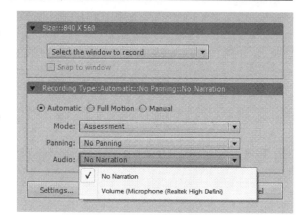

CAUTION

Recording audio while you capture may seem like a time saver, but in the long run, it may not be. It can be difficult to perform the steps and record the narration properly at the same time, meaning you may need several "takes" before getting it right. In addition, the editing process may take longer if you have to add or delete slides, change the script, etc. This option is best when you want a quick, casual sound, and use a scripted voiceover added later when you want a more polished sound.

 Recording Settings: p. 16

BRIGHT IDEAS

Setting up the Recording Environment

Microphone: Get the best results from a USB, unidirectional, headset microphone with a foam windscreen.

- The headset helps to keep the microphone a uniform distance from the speaker's mouth for a more consistent sound.

- The unidirectional feature helps eliminate background noise.

- The windscreen controls the popping and hiss sounds that come from letters such as "p" and "s."

Environment:

- Record in a room without a lot of hard, reflective surfaces such as large windows, tile floors, and metal or glass furniture. Instead, pick smaller rooms with carpet, blinds, and upholstered furniture.

- Record away from florescent lighting, electronic equipment, and air vents, which can cause background noise.

- To create a makeshift sound studio, glue "egg crate" foam sheets to a three-sided presentation board and prop it up in front of the speaker.

Tips for Audio Quality

- Before you spend a lot of time recording, timing, importing, etc., do a quick test of all the settings. Create a single-slide course, record the audio, publish it, and play it. Adjust your tone, compression settings, and other elements until you are happy with the results. Then proceed to record the rest of the audio.

- Listen to your audio using both your computer speakers and with headphones. You may notice different quality issues using each method. Consider what your users will use to help you decide if you are happy with the audio quality.

- If audio quality is extremely important to you, consider recording it outside of Captivate and then importing it. Software made specifically for audio recording (such as Audacity or Wavepad) often provide useful noise filters and more precise editing control.

Edit Audio

To edit audio:

1. Click the **Audio** menu.
2. Select **Edit**.
3. Select the audio you want to edit.
4. Make your changes in the audio editor.
5. Click the **Save** button.
6. Click the **Close** button.

To change the break points between slides:

1. Click and drag the **Slide Divider** to the point where you want it.

To delete a section of audio:

1. Click and drag your mouse in the waveform to select the audio you want to remove.
2. Click the **Delete** button.

To cut or copy and paste audio:

1. Select the audio you want.
2. Click the **Cut** or **Copy** button.
3. Click in the waveform where you want the new audio to go, or select the audio you want to replace.
4. Click the **Paste** button.

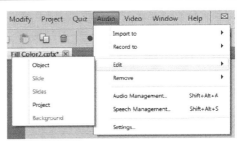

 CAUTION

If you have closed captions, editing the *project* audio will disable your closed captions and delete their timing.

 BRIGHT IDEAS

Only the **Slides** and **Project** options let you adjust the breaks between slides.

To edit the audio for one slide, just double-click the audio item in the **Timeline**.

You can edit audio in Adobe Audition right from the **Slides Audio** window, or you can edit with Soundbooth, Audition, or the software of your choice via the **Library**.

 Library, p. 184

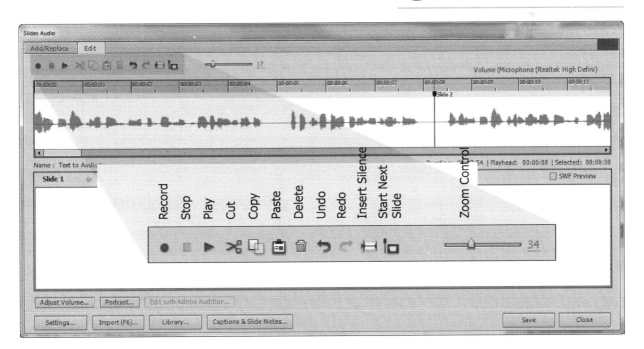

Edit Audio (continued)

To adjust volume:

1. Select the audio you want to adjust.
2. Click the **Adjust Volume** button.
3. Click and drag the **Volume** slider up to increase volume or down to decrease volume.
4. Click the **OK** button.

Audio Processing Options

Normalize: Use this option to have Captivate automatically adjust the audio to maintain a consistent volume between slides.

Dynamics: Use this option to have Captivate manage volume variations based on your settings. **Ratio** determines how loud to make the most quiet sections (2 means the volume would double.) **Threshold** determines the level of sound that shouldn't be amplified, such as background noise.

To insert silence:

1. Click in the waveform where you want the silence.
2. Click the **Insert Silence** button.
3. Enter the amount of silence you want.
4. Select the location for the silence if you want it at the start or end of the audio instead of the playhead position.
5. Click the **OK** button.

To record additional audio:

1. Click in the waveform where you want the new audio.
2. Click the **Record** button.
3. Speak into the microphone.
4. Click the **Stop** button.

To import a new audio file into the waveform:

1. Click in the waveform where you want the new audio.
2. Click the **Import** button.
3. Find and select the audio you want.
4. Click the **Open** button.

To import an audio file from the Library:

1. Click the **Library** button.
2. Select the file you want.
3. Click the **OK** button.

 The Library, p. 184

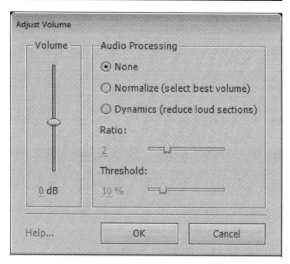

BRIGHT IDEA

One common reason to insert silence is because elements on the slide take more time to play than the audio. For example, you might try to place a slide break where the playhead is, but the break actually shows up a little bit later.

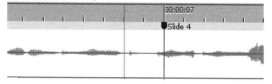

Or, you try to drag a slider to the left, and it won't go any farther.

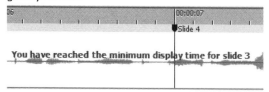

In both cases, you can insert silence to make the slide (slide 3 in these examples) longer to fit the timing better.

Export Audio

Exporting audio can be useful if you want to keep a backup of your audio, want to use it somewhere else, or need to make edits in more advanced audio editing software.

To export audio:

1. Click the **Audio** menu.
2. Select **Audio Management**.
3. Select the slides whose audio you want to export.
4. Check the boxes for the file types you want (MP3 and/or WAV).
5. Click the **Export** button.
6. Find and select the location where you want to save the audio.
7. Click the **OK** button.
8. Click the **OK** button again.

BRIGHT IDEA

You can also export the audio for the entire project. Go to the edit audio dialog box for the whole project, and click the **Podcast** button. This exports the audio into a single WAV or MP3 file.

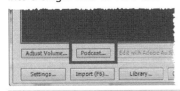

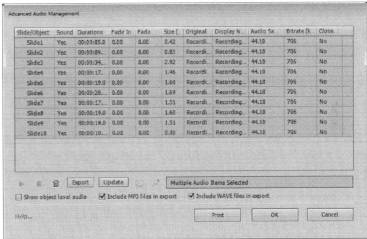

Other Audio Management Options

You are able to perform several other tasks from the **Advanced Audio Management** dialog box.

- **Play**: Select an audio file in the list at the top and click the **Play** button.
- **Remove**: Select an audio file in the list at the top and click the **Remove** button.
- **Update**: Click the **Update** button to update the audio file from the Library.
- **Add Closed Captioning**: Click the **Closed Caption** button to bring up the **Audio Editor** to the **Closed Caption** tab.
- **Edit**: Click the **Edit** button to bring up the **Audio Editor** to the **Edit** tab.

 Closed Captions, p. 80

Remove Audio

There are many ways to remove audio from a slide:

- Right-click the slide thumbnail, select **Audio**, and then **Remove**.

- Right-click the audio icon under the slide thumbnail, and click **Remove**.

- Right-click the audio in the **Timeline**, and select **Remove**.

- Click the **Remove Audio** button in the **Audio Properties** pane.

- Click the **Audio** menu, select **Remove**, and then **Slide**.

- Go to the **Advanced Audio Management** dialog box, and click the **Remove** icon.

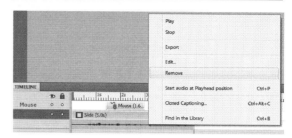

 **TIME SAVER**

You can also *edit* audio from all of these locations.

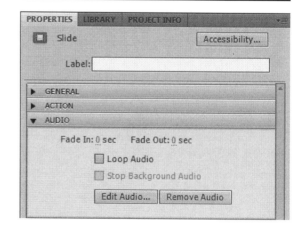

Change Settings in the Audio Pane

The **Audio** pane in the **Properties** panel has a few important slide-level settings.

- **Fade In/Fade Out**: Adjust the number if you want your audio to fade in or out—used more often with music than with voiceover.

- **Loop Audio**: Check this box if you want the audio to continue playing until the slide is done playing, even if it means playing the audio more than once—used more often with music than with voiceover. Otherwise, the audio will play only once.

- **Stop Background Audio**: If you are using background audio, check the box if you do not want it to play on this particular slide.

- **Edit Audio**: Click this button to go to the **Audio Editor**.

- **Remove Audio**: Click this button to remove the audio for the slide.

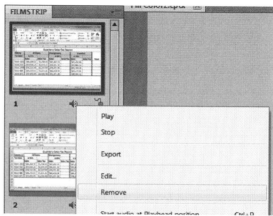

Create Audio With Text-to-Speech

To use the text-to-speech (TTS) converter, you must first install the conversion software, which is available on your installation CD if you have one or from the Adobe website.

To convert your text to speech:

1. Add your text in the **Slide Notes** panel for each slide.
2. Check the **Text-to-Speech** box next to each slide note you want to convert.
3. Click the **Text-to-Speech** button.
4. Select the voice option you want from the **Speech Agent** drop-down menu.
5. Click the **Generate Audio** button.
6. Click the **Close** button.

 Slide Notes, p. 37

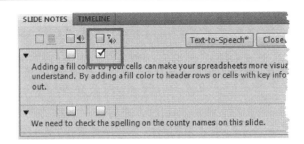

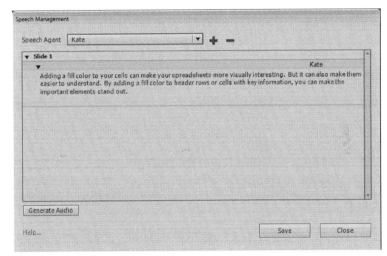

 CAUTION

If you change the text in your slide notes, the changes are NOT automatically updated in your audio. You need to regenerate the audio anytime you make changes.

 TIME SAVERS

If you'd like to generate audio for the whole project at once, go to the **Audio** menu, and select **Speech Management**. You'll see the same dialog box, but with the selected slide notes from all of your slides.

You can add/delete/edit captions right from the **Speech Management** dialog box without having to go back to the **Slide Notes** panel.

Even if you plan to use "live" narrators for the final product, consider using TTS for early drafts. That way you can make changes easily before recording the final audio.

Closed Captioning

To help make your projects accessible to people who cannot hear your audio, you can convert your slide notes into closed captions timed to that audio.

To set up closed captions, you must first have slide notes and audio for your slides. (Closed captioning options are disabled on slides without audio.) In addition, you must enable the **Closed Caption** button on the playbar for your students.

 CAUTION

If you are using closed captions, be sure to enable the **Closed Caption** button on the playbar, which is DISABLED by default. If this button is not on the playbar, your students will not be able to see the closed captions.

 Playback Control, p. 199

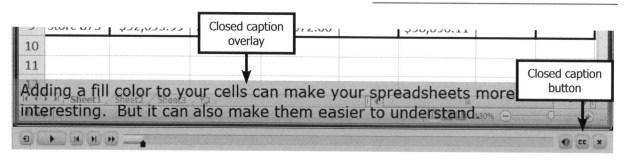

Closed caption overlay

Closed caption button

Adding a fill color to your cells can make your spreadsheets more interesting. But it can also make them easier to understand.

Create Closed Captions

To convert your slide notes to closed captions:

1. Add your text in the **Slide Notes** panel for each slide.
2. Check the **Audio CC** box next to each slide note you want to convert.
3. Click the **Closed Captioning** button.
4. Drag the caption markers in the waveform to where you want each caption to begin.
5. Click the **Save** button.
6. Click the **Close** button.

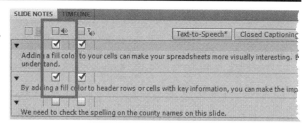

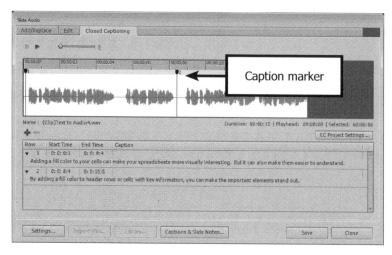

Caption marker

Change Closed Caption Settings

To change the closed captioning settings:

1. Click the **Closed Captioning** button in the **Slide Notes** panel.
2. Click the **CC Project Settings** button.
3. Change the settings you want.
4. Click the **OK** button.

Settings:

Lines: Enter a number or drag your mouse to indicate the maximum number of lines that will show at any one time. This determines the height of the closed caption overlay area.

Background: Click the color swatch to pick the color and transparency of the overlay area.

Font Settings: Select the font family, color, and size for the closed caption text.

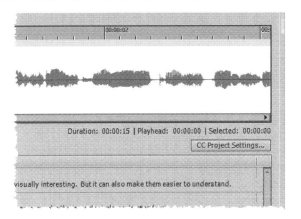

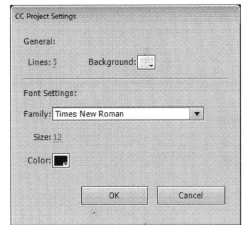

DESIGN TIP

Consider the space used by the overlay when taking your initial captures. Avoid showing anything important in the space that will be covered by the captions. Instead, position the red recording frame so that the elements being taught are shown high enough on the screen during capture.

Adding Video

Video is a great way to provide demonstrations of procedures, interviews with experts, scenarios, or visual effects.

There are two ways to add video to your projects: using the slide video method or the FLV/F4V method. Both options have their advantages as listed in the table.

Use the slide video method when you want:	Use the FLV/F4V method when you want:
• To use FLV, F4V, AVI, MP4, MOV, or 3GP movie types. • The video in the **Library**. • The video in the Table of Contents. • Closed captioning.	• To use FLV, F4V, or an online streaming service. • More than one video on the slide. • Playback controls on the video. • The video to play separately from the **Timeline**.

Add Slide Video (Flash Formats)

To add slide video using FLV or F4V format:

1. Go to the **Insert** menu.
2. Select **Slide Video**.
3. Find and select the file you want
4. Click **Open**.
5. Select the video import option you want.
6. Click **OK**.

Video Import Options:

These option only appear if your video is longer than the slide you are adding it to.

- Select the first option if you want to extend the slide to be as long as the video.

- Select the second option if you want to split the video amongst several slides, based on the current slide durations. For example, a 30-second video might be split across a 10-second slide and a 15-second slide, with the rest going on the following 20-second slide.

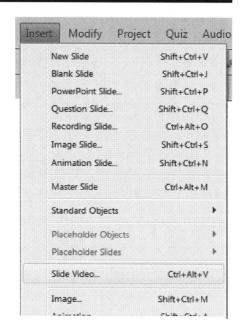

 DESIGN TIP

Once the video is on the slide, you can move, resize, rotate, and adjust timing just as with any other object.

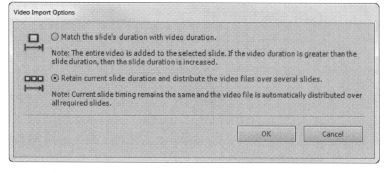

Insert Slide Video (Non-Flash Format)

If you want to import slide video using AVI, MP4, MOV, or 3GP formats, the files will to be converted to FLV format using Adobe Media Encoder (which is included with Captivate).

To add slide video using non-Flash formats:

1. Go to the **Insert** menu.
2. Select **Slide Video**.
3. Find and select the file you want.
4. Click **Open**.
5. Click the **Change Path** button if you want to store the converted video to a new location.
6. Click the **Yes** button.
7. Click **OK**.
8. Select the import option you want from the drop-down menu in the **Progress Indicator** pane.
9. Click the **Go** button.

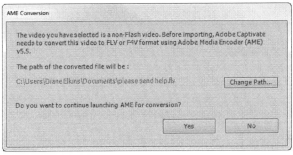

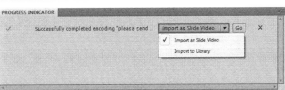

 POWER TIP

Captivate can *publish* to YouTube formats, but can you *put* a YouTube video in your project? Yes! Search Adobe Captivate Exchange for a third-party YouTube video widget.

 Widgets, p. 186

Change Slide Distribution

Whether you choose to extend the slide duration to match the video length or distribute the video across several slides, you can edit how slide video is distributed. (This option is only available when you add slide video.)

To change how the video is distributed:

1. In the **Properties** panel for the video, click the **Edit Video Timing** button.

2. Drag the black slide markers where you want the slide breaks to happen.

3. Click the **OK** button.

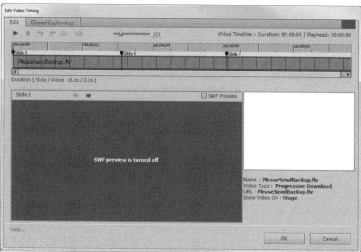

 BRIGHT IDEAS

If you drag the first marker to the left and the last marker to the right, you can include additional slides in the distribution process. In this example, the video started on slide 5. But by sliding the marker, you can now use the **Insert Previous Slide** button to include part of the video on slide 4.

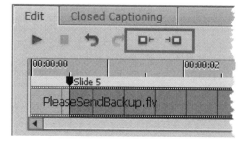

Video closed captions work very much like audio closed captions. Click the **Closed Captioning** tab to enter and time the captions.

 Closed Captioning, p. 80

Insert FLV/F4V Video

When you use the **Insert FLV/F4V File** option (as opposed to the **Insert Slide Video** option), you can either insert a file stored on your computer or a network, or you can link to a file already stored on a web server.

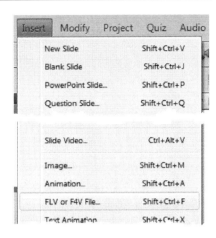

To insert FLV/F4V video from a file:

1. Go to the **Insert** menu.
2. Select **FLV or F4V File**.
3. Click the **Browse** button.
4. Find and select the file you want to use.
5. Click the **Open** button.
6. Click the **OK** button.

To insert FLV/F4V video from a web server:

1. Go to the **Insert** menu.
2. Select **FLV or F4V File**.
3. Select the **Already deployed...** radio button.
4. Enter the url for the video file.
5. Click **OK**.

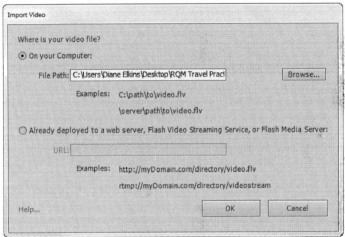

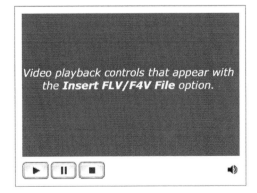

Video playback controls that appear with the Insert FLV/F4V File option.

Video Management

Video Management (available from the **Video** menu), lets you perform a number of functions:

- **Delete a video**: Select the video, and click the **Delete Session** (trash can) icon.

- **Edit the video timing**: Select the video, and click the **Edit Session** (pencil) icon.

- **Move the video to the Table of Contents**: Select the video, and then select **TOC** from the drop-down menu.

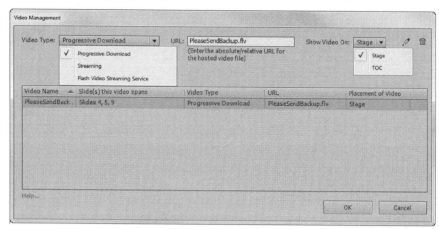

DESIGN TIP

Put the video in the table of contents (TOC) when you want the video to be the secondary visual. For example, you may have an expert explaining a process in the TOC while the main slide area shows a diagram of that process.

CAUTION

If you put a video in the table of contents, make sure you enable the TOC for your project.

 Table of Contents, p. 200

Update Project Video

If you make changes to the video, you can update your project to include the most recent version of the video.

To update project video:

1. Right-click the video in the Library.
2. Select **Update**.
3. Select the video you want to update.
4. Click the **Update** button.

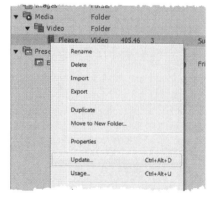

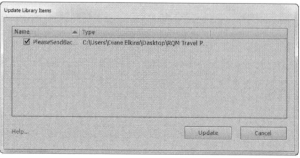

Object Properties

6

Every object has properties—every caption, every graphic, every highlight box. This chapter focuses on the properties that are common to most object types, whether sizing and rotating them, changing colors, or applying styles.

In addition to these common properties, many object types have additional properties unique to that type of object. For example, captions let you choose fonts and character formatting. You can learn more about these properties in the chapter for that object type, such as:

- Captions and other content objects, ch. 4
- Audio and video, ch. 5
- Interactive objects, ch. 7
- Questions & quizzes, ch. 10

You can find an object's properties by selecting the object in the work area or on the **Timeline**. The **Properties** panel appears on the right side of the interface by default. If you do not see the **Properties** panel, go to the **Window** menu, and select it.

In this chapter:
- Object Properties Panel
- Colors
- Object Management
- Styles
- Effects
- Timing

Notes

Object Information

Item Name

In this field, you can enter a name for each object. This is useful if you plan to have any actions for this object. When you create an action, you need to select the object from a list, and having a logical name helps you find the right object.

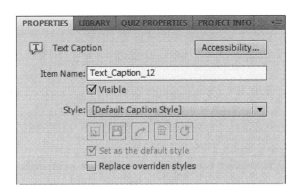

Visible

By default, all objects are visible. Uncheck this box if you want the object to be initially invisible. For example, you may create a button the student clicks to show the object.

 Actions, ch. 7

Style

The bottom half of the options in this section refer to object styles. Styles let you group formatting elements and apply them all at once.

 Object Styles, p. 98

Accessibility Button

To help make your course accessible to visually-impaired students using screen readers, click this button to add a text description of the object. This text is read to the student by the screen reader.

When the **Auto Label** box is checked, the nae of the object is used. Uncheck the box if you want to add your own text in the fields provided.

The accessibility text will only appear in your published movie if you enable accessibility for the project.

 Accessibility, p. 216

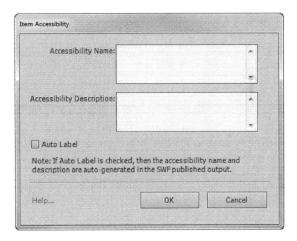

Fill & Stroke Pane

The **Fill & Stroke** pane is available on shapes, highlight boxes, and rollover objects, and hotspot areas.

Fill: Click the swatch to select the color to fill the shape.

Fill Alpha: Enter a percentage for the transparency for the fill color. 0% = transparent / 100% = opaque

Stroke: Click the swatch to select the color you want to outline the shape.

Fill Outer Area: Highlight boxes and rollover areas let you fill everything EXCEPT the shape for a spotlight effect. Check the box for this effect.

Width: Use the slider or enter the point size you want for the width of the outline.

Style: Shapes let you select the style of the outline, including **Solid**, **Dash**, **Dot**, **DashDot** and **DashDotDot**.

Corner Radius: On rectangles, you can create rounded corners by changing this value to a positive number.

Start and End: Lines let you choose what the ends of the line look like. Options include **None**, **Square**, **Round**, **Diamond**, and **Arrow**.

Highlight box and rollover area options

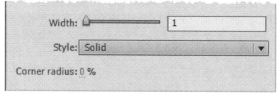

Rectangle options

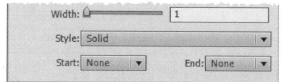

Line options

Colors

Whether you are selecting a fill color, stroke color, slide background color or any other color in Captivate, the color palette gives you many different ways to select your color.

A. Hexadecimal Value

If you know the six-digit (hexadecimal) value for the color you want, you can enter it in the text field. You can also use the text field slider to find a value close to the one entered.

B. Pre-Set Colors

Click any of the pre-set colors in the palette.

C. Recent Colors

Click any of the recently-used colors to select that color.

D. Pick Color/Eyedropper

To match a color somewhere on the screen, click the **Pick Color** button and then click on the color you want to match.

E. Color Picker

If you click the **Color Picker** button, a new window appears with additional color choices.

- Use the slider and the color area to mix any color.
- Enter HSB (hue, saturation, and brightness) values.
- Enter RGB (red, green, blue) values.
- Enter the hexadecimal (6-digit) value.

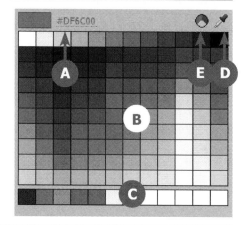

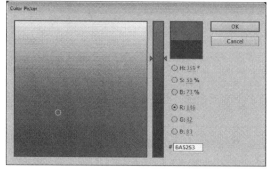

Color Gradients

When working with a slide background or a shape (rectangle, oval, etc.), the fill color palette also includes a gradient tool. Click the icon at the top of the palette to move back and forth between regular fill mode and gradient fill mode.

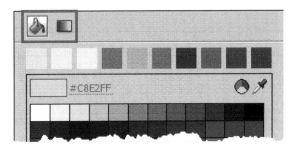

A. Pre-Made Gradients: Click an icon in the top row of swatches to use one of the pre-made gradients.

B. Direction: Click any of the swatches to change the direction of the gradient (horizontal, vertical, diagonal, etc.).

C. Custom Gradients: If you have saved any custom gradients, click the swatch to apply that gradient.

D. Gradient Bar: Use the gradient bar to customize an existing gradient or create your own.

- Click an existing color stop **(I)** to change the color for that stop.
- Click and drag a color stop to change where that color starts/stops.
- Drag a color stop away from the gradient bar to delete it.
- Click below the gradient bar to add a new color stop.

E. Linear Gradient and Radial Gradient: Click either of these icons to indicate the type of gradient you want.

F. Reverse Colors: Click this icons if you want the colors on the left to move to the right and vice-versa.

G. Add to Custom Gradients: If you create a gradient you want to use again, click this icon to add it to the Custom Gradients area. Custom gradients will be available for your other projects.

H. Remove Custom Gradients: If you want to remove one or more of your custom gradients, click this icon. This puts a small red x on each of your custom gradients. Click the red x on a gradient to delete it from your custom palette.

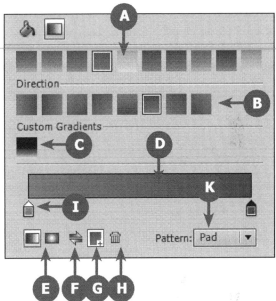

Linear Gradient

Radial Gradient

 POWER TIP

You can edit the direction of a gradient. Right-click a gradient-filled shape, and select **Edit Gradient**. This gives you a controller **(J)** you can click and drag to change the direction and the start/end points.

If the gradient is shorter than the shape, use the **Pattern** drop-down menu **(K)** to determine how to fill the remaining space.

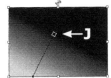

Pad *continues the end colors*

Reflect *continues the gradient in reverse*

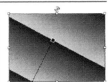

Repeat *starts the gradient over at the beginning*

Shadow Pane

You can add drop shadows to objects such as shapes, captions, and images.

Enable: Check this box to turn on the shadow.

Direction: Select **Outer** for a traditional drop shadow or **Inner** for a "sunken" effect.

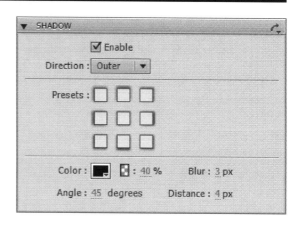

Outer shadow | *Inner shadow*

Presets: Select the angle of lighting you want, which determines on which side of the object the shadow falls.

Color: Select the color for the shadow.

Alpha: Select the alpha (opacity) of the shadow. A lower number gives you a lighter shadow, and a higher number gives you a darker shadow.

Blur: Enter a number to indicate how sharp or how blurry the edges of the shadow are. A higher number makes the shadow appear bigger.

Blur of 3 pixels | *Blur of 15 pixels*

Distance: Enter a number to determine how far away from the object you want the shadow. A larger number means it is farther away, making the object look more like it is coming off of the surface of the screen.

Distance of 4 pixels | *Distance of 15 pixels*

Angle: If you do not want to use a pre-set direction, you can indicate your own angle for the shadow.

 TIME SAVER

Many of the object properties have an **Apply to All** icon in the top-right corner of the pane. Click the icon, and then select the option you want. You can either apply the new settings to all of that type of item (all captions, all highlight boxes, etc.) or just the items that have the same style (all captions using the "incorrect" style).

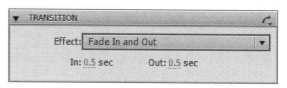

Transition Pane

The settings in the **Transition** pane determine whether an object fades in and fades out or just appears and disappears. First select the transition you want from the drop-down menu, and then use the number fields to make any fades longer or shorter.

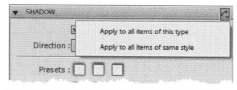

 DESIGN TIP

For a more dramatic entrance or exit (such as flying in and out), use effects instead of transitions.

Effects, p. 102

Transform Pane

The **Transform** pane lets you move, resize, and rotate objects numerically. You can also perform these same functions in the work area with your mouse.

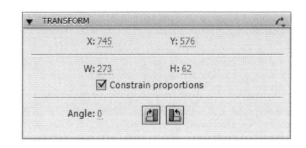

Position

X: Enter, in pixels, how far from the right edge you want the object to be.

Y: Enter, in pixels, how far from the top edge you want the object to be.

> **Mouse equivalent**: Drag the object where you want it.

Size

W: Enter, in pixels, how wide you want the object to be.

H: Enter, in pixels, how high you want the object to be.

Constrain proportions: if you check this box, when you change the value in width or height, Captivate will automatically adjust the other dimension so that the object keeps its current proportion.

> **Mouse equivalent**: Click and drag one of the side or corner handles on the object to resize it. Press and hold the **Shift** key while doing that to constrain the proportions.

 TIME SAVER

To make two or more objects the same size, use the resize tools on the **Align** toolbar.

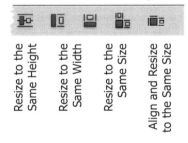

Resize to the Same Height | Resize to the Same Width | Resize to the Same Size | Align and Resize to the Same Size

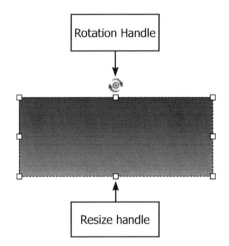

Rotation Handle

Resize handle

Rotation

Angle: Enter, in degrees, any rotation you want to give the object.

Rotate buttons: Click either the **Rotate Left** or **Rotate Right** buttons to rotate the object either direction in 90 degree increments.

> **Mouse equivalent**: Click and drag the rotation handle on top of the object. Press and hold the **Shift** key while doing that to rotate the object in 15-degree increments.

Select Objects

You can select objects either in the work area or in the **Timeline**.

Work Area

- Select a single object by clicking on it.
- Select multiple objects by holding the **Ctrl** or **Shift** key down while clicking on them, or by dragging your mouse around the objects.

Timeline

- Select a single object by clicking it in the **Timeline**.
- Select multiple objects by holding the **Ctrl** key down while clicking on them individually.
- Select consecutive items on the **Timeline** by clicking the first object, holding down the **Shift** key, and then clicking the last object.

 TIME SAVER

Click anywhere in the work area and press **Ctrl + A** to select all objects on a slide.

Cut/Copy/Paste/Duplicate Objects

You can cut, copy, and paste objects using the following methods:

- Right-click the object in the work area or the **Timeline** and select **Cut**, **Copy**, or **Paste**.
- Select the object(s) and press the keyboard shortcut shown on the right of the menu item.
- Select the object(s) and use the tools in the **Main Object** toolbar.

 TIME SAVER

Use the **Duplicate** function to copy and paste all in one step.

Delete Objects

There are several options for deleting an object.

- Select the object(s), and press the **Delete** key on your keyboard, or click the **Delete** tool on the **Main Objects** toolbar.
- Right-click the object and select **Delete**.

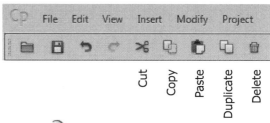

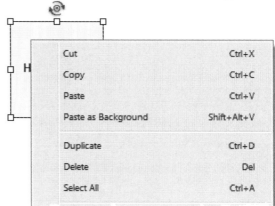

Show/Hide Objects in Edit Mode

While you are working on a slide, you can hide certain objects in the work area. This is useful when you have overlapping objects (such as a correct and incorrect caption on a quiz) and you want to more easily work with the one on the bottom.

- To hide an object in the work area, click the dot under the "eyeball" icon for that object in the **Timeline**.

- To bring an object back, click the dot again.

- Click the eyeball icon itself to show or hide all objects on the slide.

 CAUTION

Hiding an object in the **Timeline** does not change how it appears in the published movie. If you want to hide an object in a published movie, either uncheck the **Visible** check box in **Properties** or use a **Hide** action on it.

 Visibility, p. 89
Hide Actions, p. 111

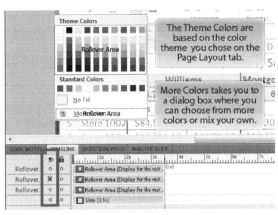

Middle rollover caption is hidden, making it easier to work with another caption it was covering.

Lock Objects in Edit Mode

When you lock an object, you cannot do ANYTHING to that object. You cannot move, edit, or delete that object. You can't even see its properties. This can be useful if you want someone else to work on certain elements of your project but not others, or you just want to keep from accidentally changing an object yourself.

- To lock an object, click the dot under the lock icon for that object in the **Timeline**.

- To unlock an object, click the dot again.

- Click the lock icon itself to lock or unlock all objects on the slide.

 BRIGHT IDEA

Remember that you can also lock the entire slide. Not only does it lock all the objects on the slide, but it keeps you from deleting the slide or changing the slide properties.

 Lock Slides, p. 42

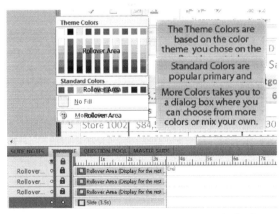

Slide with all three rollover captions locked.

Aligning Objects

You have several options for aligning objects properly on the slide to make your project look more professional.

Transform Pane

You can look at the numerical location of one object in the **Transform** pane, and then enter it into the **Transform** pane of the other object. This is the slowest of the methods on a given slide, but useful if you want to place an object in the same location on several different slides.

Alignment Toolbar

Select the objects you want, and then use the buttons on the **Align** toolbar to align them. If the **Align** toolbar isn't showing, go to the **Window** menu and select it.

These same options are available on the object's right-click menu.

Show Grid/Snap to Grid/Snap to Object

These three features can be found on the **View** menu or the **Main Object** toolbar.

Show Grid: You can show a grid on the work area to help you visually align objects. Show the grid from the **View** menu. To change the size of the grid, go to the **Edit** menu, and select **Preferences**.

Snap to Grid: In addition, you can turn on the snap feature which snaps the object into place along one of the gridlines as soon as you get close to it. This keeps you from having your objects a pixel or two off.

Snap to Object: If you want to draw a line that goes right up to the edge of another drawn object (rectangle, etc.), turn on **Snap to Object**. When you draw a line up to a shape, a small circle appears when you are right at the edge of the object. If you stop the line there, it will be perfectly lined up without a gap or overlap.

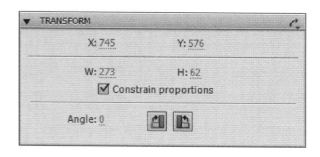

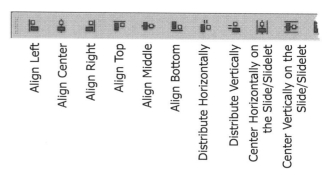

Align Left · Align Center · Align Right · Align Top · Align Middle · Align Bottom · Distribute Horizontally · Distribute Vertically · Center Horizontally on the Slide/Slidelet · Center Vertically on the Slide/Slidelet

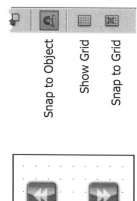

Snap to Object · Show Grid · Snap to Grid

Layering

When you have overlapping objects on a slide, you want to make sure they are layered in the right order. For example, you may want the mouse movement to go in front of a caption instead of behind it, or have a text caption appear on top of a colored box.

Drag-and-Drop Method

In the **Timeline**, the layers at the top appear in front of other layers on the slide. The layers on the bottom appear behind other objects on the slide. To change the layering order, drag and drop the layers up and down in the **Timeline**. Note that changing the top-to-bottom order in the **Timeline** does not affect when the objects appear, but rather on what layer they appear.

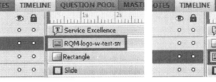

Image is in front because it is higher in the Timeline.   *Image is in back because it is lower in the Timeline.*

Right-Click and Toolbar Methods

You can access layering tools from the Main Options toolbar and the object's right-click menu, under the **Align** sub-menu.

- **Bring Forward**: Bring the selected object one layer forward (up one layer on the **Timeline**).

- **Send Backward**: Send the item back one layer (down one layer on the **Timeline**).

- **Bring to Front**: Bring the selected object to the very front layer (very top of the **Timeline**).

- **Send to Back**: Send to the very back layer (very bottom of the **Timeline**.)

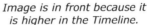
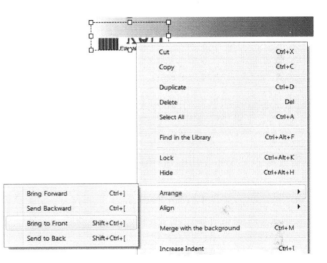

BRIGHT IDEA

Instead of having objects such as captions, images, and highlight boxes as independent objects on the slide, you can merge them into the background. When merged, they are a permanent part of the slide background and can't be moved or deleted.

Merge With Background, p. 133

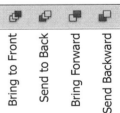

Styles

Styles are groups of format settings that can be applied all at once to an object. For example, for a caption, you can create a style that includes the caption type, font style, size, and color, etc. Styles can help you save time and create a consistent look.

You create and modify styles from the **Object Style Manager** (found on the **Edit** menu). Once it has been created, you then need to apply it to the object. For most object types, you can apply the style from the **Properties** pane for that object. With some object types, you can also apply a style from the settings for that object. For example, you can indicate the style of caption you want during a capture session from the recording settings dialog box.

Styles can be created for:

Standard Objects	Quizzing Objects
• Captions (text, rollover, success, failure, and hint) • Text entry boxes • Text entry box buttons • Highlight boxes • Rollover areas • Rollover slidelets (rollover area and slidelet) • Zoom area (zoom source and zoom destination)	• Captions (correct, incorrect, retry, timeout, incomplete, advance feedback, title, question text, answer/FIB text, header (matching/ likert), matching entries, likert question, scoring result, scoring result label) • Buttons (skip, back, continue, submit, clear, review, retake) • Progress indicator • Review area • HotSpot • Short Answer

Modify an Existing Style

All object types come with at least one style—the default styles. You can modify that default style and any custom styles from the **Object Style Manager**.

1. Click the **Edit** menu.
2. Select **Object Style Manager**.
3. In the pane on the left, select the type of object you want to modify.
4. In the pane in the middle, select the specific style you want to modify.
5. In the panes on the right, make the formatting changes you want.
6. Click **OK**.

The options on the right vary based on the object type, and are many of the same options you'll find on that object's **Properties** pane.

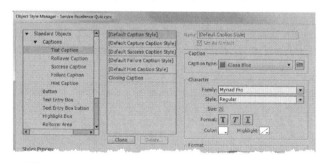

 BRIGHT IDEA

If you make any changes to styles while you are in a project, the style changes affect only that project. But if you modify styles with no project open, the style changes will be available in all future projects.

Create a New Style

To create a new style:

1. Click the **Edit** menu.

2. Select **Object Style Manager**.

3. In the pane on the left, select the type of object you want to modify.

4. In the pane in the middle, select a style that is most similar to the style you want to create.

5. Click the **Clone** button.

6. In the **Name** field, type the name for the new style.

7. In the panes on the right, make the formatting changes you want.

8. Click **OK**.

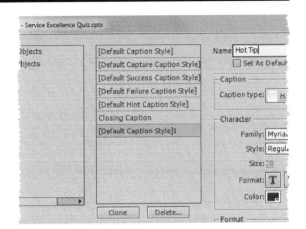

Set the Default Style

The default style is the style used when an object is first created. For example, when you create a new highlight box or button, it first appears on your slide in the default style.

To change the default style, you can go to the **Object Style Manager**, select the default style, and modify it. Or, you can create a new style and then designate it as the default.

To designate the default:

1. Click the **Edit** menu.

2. Select **Object Style Manager**.

3. In the pane on the left, select the type of object you want to work with.

4. In the pane in the middle, select the style you want to use for the default.

5. Check the **Set as Default** box.

6. Click **OK**.

Now when you create a new object of that type, it will automatically have that new style.

 BRIGHT IDEA

You can also change the defaults from **Preferences** (on the **Edit** menu).

Apply Styles to an Object

To apply a style to an object:

1. Select that object on the slide.
2. Click the **Properties** tab.
3. Select the **Style** from the drop-down menu.

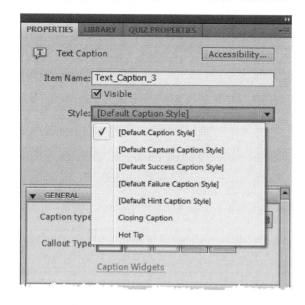

Additional Style Options

If you make any changes to an object's style-related properties (caption type, fill color, font, etc.), you get some additional style options in the **Properties** pane.

Create New Style: Rather than going to the **Object Style Manager**, you can create a new style right here. Format your object on the slide, and then click this button to create a new style based on that object. For example, if you have a highlight box with a red border, you can give one a blue border and save that as a new style.

Save Changes to Existing Style: Instead of making a new style from your revised object, you can overwrite that style with the new changes. For example, if your font isn't big enough, you can change the size and resave the style.

Apply this style to: If you change the style of an object, you can apply it to all other objects in the project with any given style. For example, you can apply your new green caption style to all of the objects that currently use the blue caption style.

Delete style: Click this button to delete the style from the project.

Reset Style: If you have made changes to the object, click this button if you want to reapply the original style.

Replace Overridden Style: If you change the style-related properties of an object, it is considered overridden. Overridden objects have a plus sign next to the name of the style. If you make changes to a style, it does not apply to any objects that are overridden, unless you check this box.

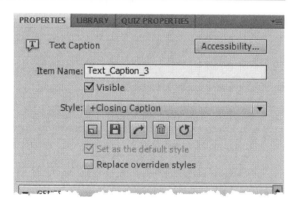

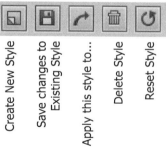

Import and Export Styles

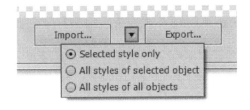

If you are working on a team, you can share styles with teammates so you have a consistent look, and you don't all have to set up the styles yourself. You can also import and export project-specific styles from one project to another.

To export styles:

1. Click the **Edit** menu.
2. Select **Object Style Manager**.
3. Click the arrow next to the **Export** button.
4. Select the option for which styles you want to export.
5. Click the **Export** button.
6. Navigate to where you want to save the style.
7. Click **Save**.
8. Click **OK**.

To import styles:

1. Click the **Edit** menu.
2. Select **Object Style Manager**.
3. Click the **Import** button.
4. Find and select the style (.cps) you want to import.
5. Click **Open**.
6. Click **OK**.

BRIGHT IDEA

Remember that if you manage styles with a project open, the changes affect that project only. If you manage styles with no projects open, then it affects all future projects.

Delete Styles

To delete a style:

1. Click the **Edit** menu.
2. Select **Object Style Manager**.
3. In the pane on the left, select the type of object you want to delete.
4. In the pane in the middle, select the specific style you want to delete.
5. Click the **Delete** button.
6. If there are no objects in the project using that style, that's all you need to do. If, however, there are any objects in the project that use that style, you need to choose what style you want to give them instead.
7. Select the style you want from the drop-down menu.
8. Click **OK**.

Object Effects

Object effects let you create visual interest as objects appear, disappear, or move across the slide, similar to animations in PowerPoint. Effects in Captivate can either happen based on the **Timeline** (fly in at 3.5 seconds) or based on an action (the page loading or the student clicking a button).

Effects are managed in the **Effects** panel. To show the **Effects** panel, go to the **Window** menu, and select **Effects**.

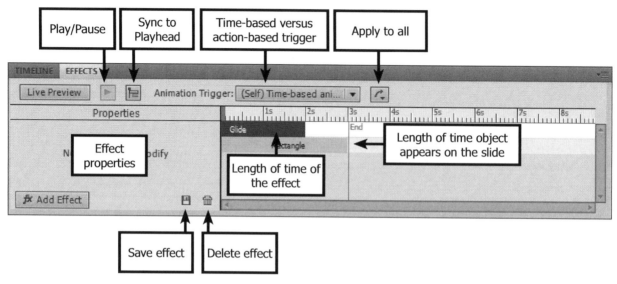

Play/Pause

Sync to Playhead

Time-based versus action-based trigger

Apply to all

Effect properties

Length of time object appears on the slide

Length of time of the effect

Save effect

Delete effect

Add a Time-Based Effect

Time-based effects start and end based on specified points in the **Timeline**. When you go to the **Effects** panel for a given object, that object appears in the effects **Timeline** for the amount of time that object appears on the main **Timeline**. In the example above, the rectangle is up on the slide for three seconds, so its effects **Timeline** is also 3 seconds. That is the maximum amount of time you have to work with for effects. If you wanted an object to have a five-second effect, then you would first need to extend that object to at least five seconds in the main **Timeline**.

To add a time-based effect:

1. Select the object you want to add the effect to.
2. Click the **Effects** tab.
3. Click the **Add Effect** button.
4. Select the effect you want.
5. Move and resize the effect item on the **Timeline** to change the starting time, ending time, and duration.
6. Repeat steps 3-5 for additional effects for that object.

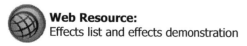 **Web Resource:**
Effects list and effects demonstration

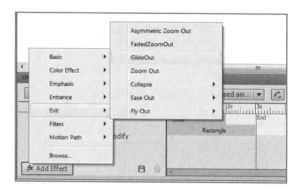

 BRIGHT IDEA

Some effects have properties that let you customize the effect. For example, the blur filter lets you indicate how much of a blur effect you want. When an object has options, they appear in the **Properties** section of the **Effects** panel.

Add an Action-Based Effect

Setting up an action-based effect starts with the trigger, meaning the item that will trigger the event. For example, if you wanted the animation to start when the student clicks a button, then you would start with the button. You'll have to determine what object you want to use as the trigger as well as the specific action you want to use for the trigger. For example, on a button, you might want to trigger the effect on success or after the last unsuccessful attempt.

To add an action-based effect:

1. Select the object that will trigger the effect.
2. In the **Actions** pane for that object, click the drop-down menu for the trigger you want.
3. Select **Apply Effect**.
4. Click the **Object Name** drop-down menu that appears.
5. Select the object you want to apply the effect to.
6. Click the **[...]** button to go to the object that will have the effect (or simply select that object in the work area).
7. In the **Effects** panel, click the **Animation Trigger** drop-down menu.
8. Select the name of the action that will initiate the trigger.
9. Add your effect. (See steps 3-5 on previous page.)

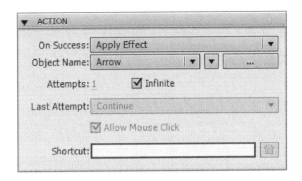

 Actions, ch. 7

![Power Tip icon] **POWER TIP**

In addition to the effects that come with Captivate, you can also create your own effects in Flash and bring them in to Captivate. Search Adobe Help for "Creating custom effects in Adobe Flash for specific guidelines."

Managing Effects

Preview Effects

Effects do not show up when you preview just the single slide. Instead, you can use the other standard preview mode (such as **Next 5 slides**), or you can preview from the **Effects** panel.

To preview effects, click the **Live Preview** button. From there, you can use the playhead and the **Play/Pause** button to view the animation. Then click the **Edit View** button to return to edit mode.

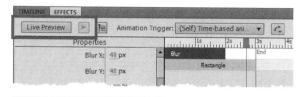

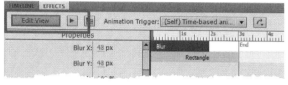

Remove an Effect

To remove an effect, select the effect in the **Effects Timeline**, and click the **Delete** (trash can) button.

Sync to Playhead

This button lets you determine when an effect will take place on the main slide. On the *effects* **Timeline**, put the playhead where you want it, and click the **Sync to Playhead** button. This takes you to the *slide* **Timeline**, putting the playhead in the corresponding spot. For example, 2.5 seconds on the *effects* **Timeline** might correspond to 7 seconds on the *slide* **Timeline**.

Save and Reuse Effects

You can reuse effects for a given object (so that you don't have to set them up over and over again. Effects are saved as XML files. All time-based effects for that object are included in the file.

To save an object's effects:
1. Select the object with the effects.
2. In the **Effects** panel, click the **Save** button.
3. Designate a name and location for the file.
4. Click the **Save** button.

To reuse a saved effect:
1. Select the object you want to give the effects to.
2. Click the **Add Effect** button.
3. Select **Browse**.
4. Find and select the saved effects file.
5. Click the **Open** button.

Motion Paths

When you add a motion path, you can configure the individual points on the path. For example, if you have a left-to-right motion path, you can modify the path to be a certain length or angle.

To modify a motion path:
1. Click the small icon that appears to the bottom-right of the object.
2. Click and drag any of the points on the arrow.

POWER TIP

Reused effects are also available for use with advanced actions.

Advanced Actions, ch. 9

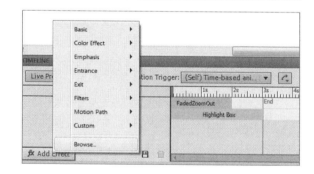

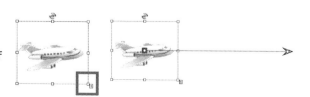

Timing Slide Objects

A Captivate project plays like a movie along the **Timeline**. Once your objects are on the slide, you'll want to time them to appear in the appropriate sequence and to stay on-screen for the appropriate length of time. For example, a caption needs to stay up long enough to be read, and a highlight box or image might need to appear at a certain point in the audio, if you have any.

On the **Timeline** for each slide, you can quickly adjust the start, duration, and finish of each slide object as well as the length of the slide as a whole.

 CAUTION

When a slide is finished playing, the movie automatically goes on to the next slide. If you want the student to choose when to advance to the next slide, you'll need to add a button or other object that pauses the slide until the student clicks it.

 Buttons, p. 116

Adjust Timing of Slide Elements

To adjust timing on the Timeline tab:

1. Drag the left edge of an item to adjust the start time.

2. Drag the right edge of an item to adjust the end time.

3. Drag the entire object to move it to a different place on the **Timeline**.

To adjust timing in the Properties panel:

1. Select the object in the **Timeline** or the work area.

2. In the **Timing** pane, enter the duration for the object in **Display For** field.

3. Enter the start time in the **Appear After** field.

Timing Options

The **Display For** drop-down menu has some additional timing options.

- **Specific time**: This is the default. This displays the caption for the amount of time set in the **Timeline** or in the Timing pane.

- **Rest of slide**: This extends the caption to the end of the slide and "locks" it in place so that if the slide is extended, the object is extended as well.

- **Rest of project**: This extends the caption to the end of the project. The object will only appear on this slide's **Timeline**, but will show up on every other slide for the rest of the project.

 **Web Resource:**
Timing Objects Screencast

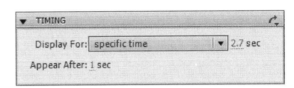

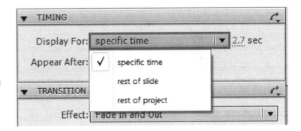

 BRIGHT IDEA

- If your **Timeline** isn't showing, go to the **Window** menu, and select **Timeline**.

- Use the zoom control to zoom the **Timeline** in or out for more or less detail.

Notes

Actions & Interactions 7

Actions are commands that can either be triggered by the student (such as clicking a button) or triggered automatically (such as reaching the end of a slide). Actions let you customize the functionality of the course and make it more interactive.

In this chapter, you will learn first about the individual action options. Once you understand the capabilities of the various actions, they become building blocks that let you build any number of features from branching navigation to games. Then you will learn about the objects that trigger those actions, such as a button the student can click to launch a document.

Some interactive objects come with a pre-set action, while others can be set up with the action of your choice The following table describes the action options for the various trigger objects.

Object	Action options
Slide	Even though this technically isn't an interactive object, you can assign an action for when the slide starts and finishes.
Click Box	Select one action for clicking/answering successfully and/or one action for failing to click/answer successfully after the specified number of attempts.
Button	
Text Entry Box	
Quiz Question	
Rollover Caption	A text caption appears when the student rolls over the hot spot.
Rollover Image	An image appears when the student rolls over the hot spot.
Rollover Slidelet	A mini slide (with text, graphics, audio, etc.) appears when the student rolls over the hot spot area. You can add an additional action for when the student clicks the hot spot.

Many properties for interactive objects are the same as for other objects (such as size, layering, and shadows). This chapter explains the properties specific to the interactivity. Refer to the Objects chapter for information on the standard properties. Quiz questions are covered in the Questions & Quizzes chapter.

Object Properties, ch. 6
Questions & Quizzes, ch. 10

Notes

Action Types

Objects that serve as triggers for an action have an **Action** pane in the **Properties** panel. The available actions vary somewhat based on the type of object you are applying it to.

Continue: Continue to play along the **Timeline**. This action is useful if the action is paused, perhaps because of a click box or button.

Go To and Jump Actions: These actions allow for custom navigation and branching.

> **Go to the previous slide**: Go to the beginning of the previous slide.
>
> **Go to the next slide**: Go to the beginning of the next slide
>
> **Go to the slide last visited**: Go to the beginning of the slide the student was on before the current slide.
>
> **Jump to slide**: Go to the beginning of the slide specified in the **Action** pane.

Open URL or file: Go to a webpage or link to a file.

> Go to a webpage (such as a page on your website or a PDF document stored on your intranet). For this action, type the URL in the space provided.
>
> Link to a file (such as a file on your computer or a network drive). Click the **Browse** button **(A)** to find and select the file you want to link to. When you use this option, the file needs to be included with the published movie, or the link will not work.
>
> For both options, click the drop-down menu **(B)** to indicate how you want the webpage or file to open.
>
> > **Current**: Webpage or document replaces the Captivate movie in the current browser window.
> >
> > **New**: Webpage or document opens in a new browser window.
> >
> > **Parent and Top**: These only apply if your movie will play on a webpage with frames. **Parent** replaces all the frames in the current frameset, while **Top** opens the webpage or document in the topmost frame.
> >
> > With all but the **Current** option, you can check the box at the bottom to indicate whether you want the movie to continue playing once the new -webpage launches.

Open another project: Open a Captivate project file, template, or published movie. Click the **Browse** button to find and select the file, and click the drop-down arrow to indicate how you want the new file to open. You can use this action for any of the following file types:

- Captivate project file (.cptx or .cp)
- Captivate template file (.cptl)
- RoboDemo file (.rd)
- Flash output file (.swf)

 CAUTION

Don't confuse the following actions:

> Imagine the student is on slide 3 and then goes to slide 6. **Go to the previous slide** takes the student to slide 5. **Go to the last slide visited** takes the student back to slide 3.
>
> With a **Continue** action, the project keeps playing from that point in the Timeline. With a **Go to the next slide** action, it goes immediately to the next slide and does not finish the slide it is on.

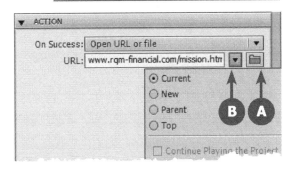

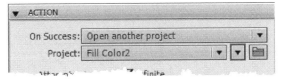

Action Types (continued)

Send E-Mail to: Open the student's default e-mail program with a message addressed to the address entered in the **Action** pane. Click the drop-down arrow to indicate if you want to continue playing the project or you want to pause the project when the e-mail message opens.

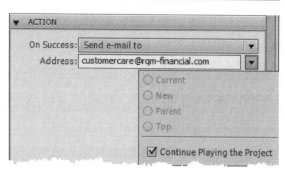

 CAUTION

Be sure to test the e-mail function carefully in your environment. The configuration of the user's computer and your servers can cause complications.

Execute JavaScript: Run JavaScript code entered in the **Action** pane. This lets you extend the capabilities of what Captivate can do. For example, you could:

- Manipulate something on the HTML page from within Captivate.
- Create a custom pop-up message window.
- Communicate with other Captivate movies.

To enter your code, click the Script Window button, enter your code, and click the **OK** button.

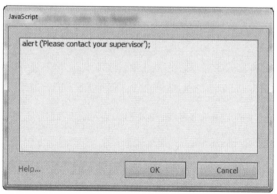

 BRIGHT IDEAS

If you don't know JavaScript, you can often find sample code in the Captivate forum or blogs.

JavaScript is interpreted by a browser, so use the **In Web Browser** preview mode to test your work.

Execute Advanced Actions: Advanced actions let you perform more than one action at once, use conditional actions (only perform an action if something is true), or build customized actions. After you build the advanced action in the **Advanced Actions** dialog box, then you run it with this action.

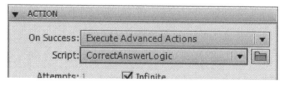

 Advanced Actions, ch. 9

Action Types (continued)

Show: Make a hidden object visible. This is used with objects whose visibility has been turned off in its **Properties** panel. For example, if you want to add a hint to a quiz question, place a text box on the page and make it invisible. Then create a **Hint** button with the **Show** action that shows the hint text caption.

Hide: Make a visible object invisible. For example, you might want the student to click a button to make an image disappear, revealing information beneath it.

 BRIGHT IDEA

- It's a good idea to name your objects in the **Properties** panel. That makes it easier to find the one you want when you have to select it from a drop-down menu.

- Remember that if you just need to show and hide objects based on time, you can simply adjust their placement on the **Timeline**. Use the **Show** and **Hide** actions if you want them to appear and disappear based on a student click, based on if/then conditions, etc.

Enable: Activate an interactive object (such as a button or click box) that has previously been disabled. For example, you might want to have the **Next** button disabled until certain tasks are performed or conditions met. Once those conditions are met, then the button could be enabled.

Disable: De-activate an interactive object (such as a button or click box). The object will still be visible on the screen, but associated actions will not work.

With **Enable** and **Disable**, select the object you want to enable/disable from the drop-down menu that appears. Only eligible objects appear on the drop-down menu.

Variable-Based Actions:

Assign: Set the variable to the value indicated.

Increment: Add an amount to the variable.

Decrement: Subtract an amount from the variable.

 Variables, p. 139

Apply Effect: Execute a special effect such as a motion path or fly-in effect on an object.

 Action-Based Effects, p. 103

No Action: Do nothing.

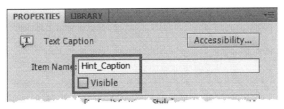

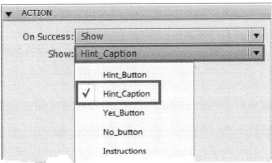

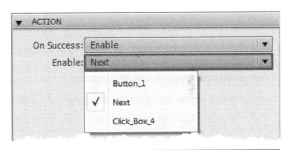

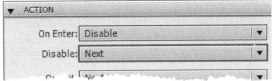

 DESIGN TIP

What's the point of setting up an action that does nothing?!? This is often used for objects, such as a button or click box where there is one option on success and one option for failure, and you don't need both options.

DESIGN TIPS

Creating Branching Scenarios

In a branching scenario, the student makes choices that determine where he or she goes next. For example, in a customer service scenario, the student can choose between several options. Each option takes the student to a different slide for feedback and a continuation of the scenario.

To create a branching scenario, it is usually best to sketch it out first. This will help you make your basic design decisions before you build it.

- Do you want to give students the chance to go back and change their answers?
- After getting feedback, do all students go to the same question next, or do they get different questions based on their responses?
- How many content slides do you need for instructions and to set up the scenario?
- Can the new question be on the same slide as the feedback for the previous question, or do you need separate slides?

Once you have your structure in place, give names to all of the slides. This will make it easier to "connect" them in Captivate.

Then, set up the structure before adding content. Create and name your slides, and then set up your actions (using quiz questions, regular slides with buttons, etc.). Once you have the logic working, then you can add your content.

Using Branching View

To help you manage the flow of slides in any project with branching, you can use the branching view. Branching view is a flowchart-style view that helps you quickly determine where the student can go from each of the slides.

To show branching view:

1. Go to the **Window** menu.
2. Select **Branching View**.

From branching view, you can:

- Create and manage slide groups. **(A)**
- Export the view as a bitmap. **(B)**
- View or change the action of an interactive object. **(C)** Click the navigation line for the action box to appear.
- View success, failure, and navigational paths. **(D)**
- Expand and collapse sections. **(E)**
- View or change the action of a slide. **(F)** Click a thumbnail for the action box to appear.

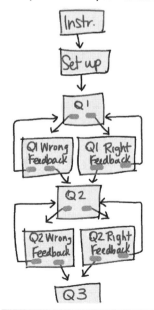

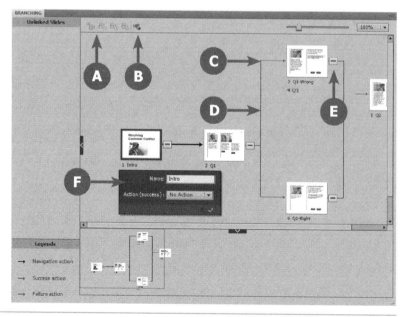

Add Actions to a Slide

Actions can be triggered when the project goes to the first frame of a slide (**On Enter**) or the last frame of the slide (**On Exit**). For example, you might want to run an advanced action at the end of the slide that branches to different slides based on whether or not the student is a supervisor.

To add an action to a slide:

1. Select the slide(s) you want in the **Filmstrip**.
2. Select the action from the **On Enter** and/or **On Exit** menus in the **Action** pane.

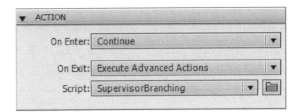

 CAUTION

An **On Exit** action will only execute if the project reaches the last frame of the slide. It will not execute if the student leaves the slide in the middle, such as by clicking a button that takes them to the next slide.

Add a Click Box

Click boxes are useful for turning images into hotspots. For example, you can show three images, each with a click box over them. Each of the click boxes could link to a slide with more information.

Click boxes can have success and failure captions as well as success and failure actions.

To add a click box:

1. Click the **Insert Click Box** tool in the **Toolbar**.

Click Box Properties

Action Pane

On Success: Select an action that executes if the student clicks in the click box.

Attempts: Enter the number of attempts the student gets before the interaction is considered incorrect. Either enter a number in the **Attempts** number field or check the Infinite check box.

Last Attempt: Select an action that executes if the student fails to click inside the click box within the specified number of attempts.

Allow Mouse Click and **Shortcut**: Click boxes are designed to be...clicked! However, sometimes you might want to test the student on a keystroke command. There is not a designated Captivate object for that, but you can use a click box object for it.

- Type the keyboard shortcut in the **Shortcut** field.

- If you want the student to be able to use either the keyboard shortcut or a click in the click box as the correct action, then leave the **Allow Mouse Click** box checked. If you only want to consider the keyboard shortcut as correct, uncheck the box.

- To clear the **Shortcut** field, click the **Clear** (trash can) button.

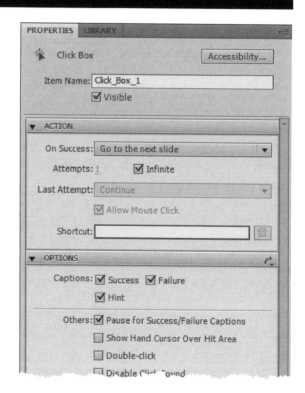

Options Pane

Captions: Check the boxes for whichever captions you want to include with the click box.

- **Success** shows when the student clicks in the click box (or presses the corresponding keyboard shortcut).

- **Failure** shows when the student clicks somewhere other than the clickbox. If you have more than one clickbox on the slide, test your design to make sure it operates as intended.

- **Hint** shows up when the student's mouse hovers over the click box area.

 CAUTION

Be sure to test any keyboard shortcuts in a web browser to make sure the project shortcuts don't interfere with any web browser shortcuts.

Click Box Properties (continued)

Others

Pause for Success/Failure Captions: Success and failure captions are not in the **Timeline**. If you include these captions, you'll need to decide if you want the project to pause long enough to read them or if you want the captions to appear while the project continues. The project pauses by default. Uncheck the box if you don't want the project to pause.

Show Hand Cursor Over Hit Area: Check this box if you want the student's cursor to change from an arrow to a hand when it is over the click box area. This is an indication to the student that the cursor is over a hot spot area.

Double-Click: Check this box if you want the student to double-click the box instead of single-click the box. This is most commonly used in computer simulations.

Disable Click Sound: When a student clicks the click box, Captivate plays a click sound. Check this box if you don't want the sound to play.

Pause Project Until User Clicks: When there is a click box on the screen, the project pauses until the student either clicks successfully in the box or uses up all of the incorrect attempts. Uncheck the box if you don't want to pause the project.

Right-Click: Check this box if you want the student to right-click the box instead of the traditional left-click. This is most commonly used in computer simulations.

Reporting Pane

Include in Quiz: Check this box if you want to count the click box interaction as a question in a quiz.

Points: Enter the number of points for clicking the click box correctly in the specified number of attempts. The value can be between 0 and 100.

Add to Total: Check this box if you want to include the points in the quiz total.

Report Answers: Check this box if you want to send the scores to a learning management system (LMS). Uncheck it if the score does not need to be reported.

Interaction ID: Enter an ID to be used when sending the data to the LMS. This can help you identify the data in the LMS.

 LMS Reporting, p. 206

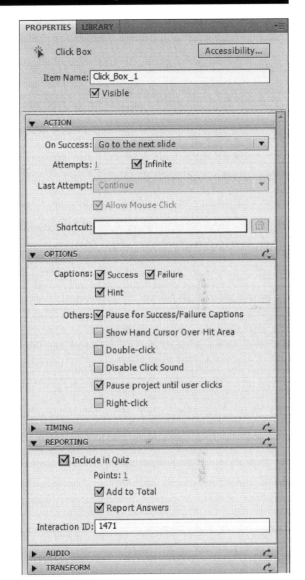

Add a Button

Buttons are a very flexible way to add interactivity, because there are so many ways you can format them. Use buttons for course navigation, branching scenarios, questions built outside of the question wizard, pop-up interactions, etc.

Buttons can have success and failure captions as well as success and failure actions. However, the captions are turned off by default.

To add a button:

1. Click the **Insert Button** tool in the **Toolbar**.

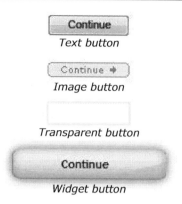

Text button

Image button

Transparent button

Widget button

Button Properties

Most of the button properties are the same as the properties for a click box. This section covers the properties that are different.

 Click Box Properties, p. 114

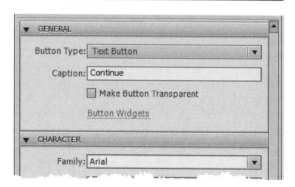

Button Type: Select from the following options:

Text Buttons: Type the text for the button in the **Caption** field. Format the text in the **Character** pane.

Transparent Button: Use the **Fill & Stroke** pane to change the button's fill color and transparency and stroke color and weight. A transparent button works very similarly to a click box.

Image Button: Select a button from the options provided, or click the **Browse** button to select your own.

Make Button Transparent: Check this box to make the background of a text button transparent.

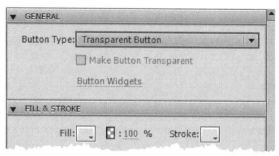

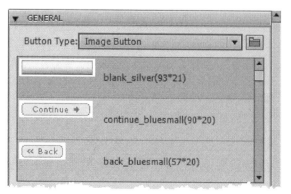

Button Widgets

Button widgets offer additional button formats and effects. The button widgets come in two forms:

- **Interactive**: Interactive buttons have the same basic action properties as a regular button: action on success, action on failure, and success, failure, and hint captions.
- **Static**: Static buttons have a single action, no failure action, and no captions.

To add a button from the button widgets:

1. Click the **Insert Button** tool in the **Toolbar**.

2. In the **Properties** pane, click the **Button Widgets** link. **(A)**

3. In the **Widgets** panel, click **Insert** for either the **Static** or **Interactive** button. **(B)**

4. In the **Widget Properties** dialog box **(C)**, select the options including the success action and button text.

5. Click the **OK** button.

To make changes later, click the **Widget Properties** button in the **Properties** panel. **(D)**

For interactive buttons, use the **Action** and **Options** panes to configure the attempts, captions, etc.

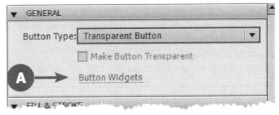

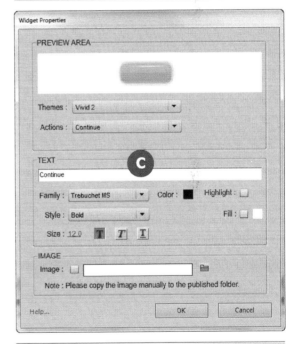

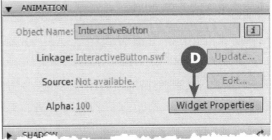

Add a Text Entry Box

Text entry boxes let the student enter text. This text can then be validated (graded), sent to the LMS, or stored and used later for conditional logic or to display back to the student. Remember that you can also use a fill-in-the-blank question for similar purposes.

Text entry boxes can have success and failure actions and captures.

To add a text entry box:

1. Click the **Insert Text Entry Box** tool in the **Toolbar**.

Text Entry Box Properties

General Pane

Default Text: By default, the text entry box appears blank to the student. But you can enter text here to appear in the text box for the student. For example, if you have a field for the person's name, you can add default text that says "Enter name here." This text is editable by the student.

Retain Text: By default, the student's answer stays in the text box if the student navigates away from the page and returns during the same session. Uncheck the box if you want the answer cleared when the student leaves the page.

Show Text Box Frame: By default, there is an outline around the entry box. Uncheck the box if you don't want the frame. For example, if you are laying the text box over a shape, you may not need the frame.

Password Field: If you are using the entry box as a password field (or to simulate one), check this box. Then the student's typing is captured as typed but is shown as asterisks.

Validate User Input: By default, a text entry box is not graded. However, if you want to grade the answer, check this box. When you do, a small dialog box appears that lets you add one or more correct answers.

Var Associated: A variable is a stored piece of data. All text entry boxes are assigned a variable, letting you capture the student's entry and use it later, if needed. You can either use the variable name provided, select a variable that already exists from the drop-down menu, or click the **X** button to create a new variable name.

 Variables, p. 139

On Focus Lost: Select an action to execute when the student clicks off of the text entry box.

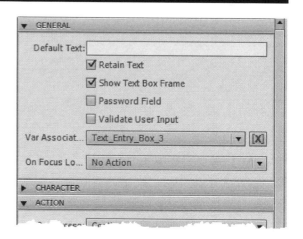

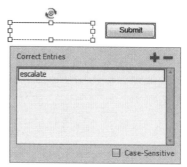

Text Entry Box Properties (continued)

Action Pane

The **Action** pane for a text entry box is similar as for other interaction objects. The main difference how the **Shortcut** field works. By default, text entry boxes come with a shortcut of **Enter**.

With non-validated text entry boxes (and most other interactive objects), the keyboard shortcut activates the **On Success** action. But for text boxes that are validated, this shortcut is what triggers the validation. Then the grading logic (**On Success** action, number of attempts, etc.) is activated.

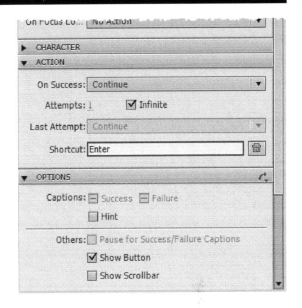

Options Pane

Captions: The success and failure options are only available if you are validating the student's entry. Check the **Hint** box if you want a hint caption to appear when the student hovers over the text entry box. This can be useful for instructions.

Show Button: By default, a **Submit** button is added with your text entry box, used to validate the student's input. Uncheck this box if you don't want such a button, for example, if you want to use the keyboard shortcut for validation or don't have any validation. You can click the button itself to change its properties.

Show Scrollbar: Check this box if you want to add a scrollbar to the text box, letting the student enter more text in a smaller amount of space.

Rollover Objects

The three types of rollover objects let you quickly create interactive objects where students roll their mouse over a hot spot to reveal additional content.

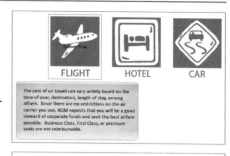

- **Rollover Captions**: Place hotspots on the slide that the student rolls over to view a text caption.

- **Rollover Image**: Place hotspots on the slide that the student rolls over to view an image.

- **Rollover Slidelets**: Place hotspots on the slide that the student rolls over to view a mini-slide that can contain text, images, audio, etc.

Web Resource:
Screencast: Rollover Object Options

Insert a Rollover Caption

To add a rollover caption:

1. Click the **Insert Rollover Caption** tool.

2. Move and resize the rollover area over the area to serve as the hot spot for the caption.

3. Move and resize the caption and enter the pop-up text.

4. Repeat steps 1-3 for additional rollover captions.

5. Format the objects in the **Properties** panel.

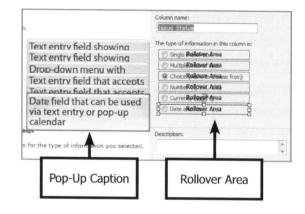

Pop-Up Caption   Rollover Area

 TIME SAVER

If you are placing the rollover area over an object, such as an image, you can save yourself a little bit of time. Right-click the rollover area and select **Auto-adjust Rollover Area**. This "snaps" the rollover area to the same size as the object below it, so that you don't have to resize it manually. (This method is not helpful if the Rollover Area is on top of just a part of the underlying object.)

 CAUTION

Your movie will not automatically stop so that students can roll over all of the hotspots and read all of the text. To give them enough time, either extend the length of the slide, or add a **Continue** button that pauses the slide until they want to continue.

 Buttons, p. 116

Insert a Rollover Image

To add a rollover image:

1. Go to the **Insert** menu.
2. Select **Standard Objects**.
3. Select **Rollover Image**.
4. Find and select the image you want to use.
5. Click the **Open** button.
6. Format and position the rollover area and the image.

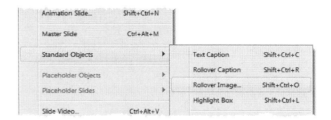

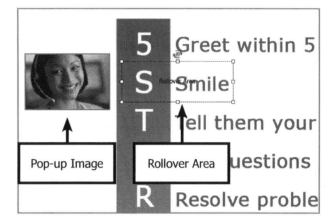

Pop-up Image   Rollover Area

! CAUTION

It's easy to forget about rollover images because it is the only standard object that is not on the **Object** toolbar. You can only access it from the **Insert** menu.

💡 BRIGHT IDEA

The rollover objects do not require a mouse, making them accessible. When a student using a screen reader or keyboard navigation tabs to the rollover area, the caption, image, or slidelet appears (as opposed to click objects, where the student must press **Enter** before the action is triggered).

Insert a Rollover Slidelet

To add a rollover slidelet:

1. Click the **Insert Rollover Slidelet** button.

2. Move and resize the rollover slidelet area over the area to serve as the hot spot for the slidelet.

3. Move and resize the slidelet frame to the size and location you want.

4. Format the two objects as needed.

5. Select the slidelet in the work area.

6. Add objects to the slidelet as you would to a regular slide.

The slidelet has its own **Timeline**. To add objects to the slidelet, the slidelet's **Timeline** must be showing. Do this by selecting the slidelet object on the main slide.

Objects as they first appear on the slide

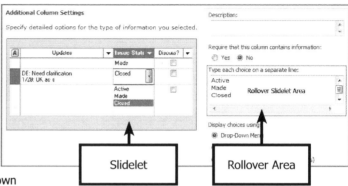

Slidelet   Rollover Area

Rollover Area Properties

Both the rollover area and the slidelet have their own properties. Most of the properties are the same as for any other object type. However, the rollover area for a slidelet has some additional properties. **(A)**

Show Runtime Border: If you select this option, a border appears around the rollover area while the student's mouse is over it. This is useful when you have more than one on a slide as it lets the student know which object they are viewing.

Stick Slidelet: By default, the slidelet disappears when the student rolls off the rollover area. If you check this box, the slidelet stays up. A close button appears on the slidelet that the student would click to close it.

On Click: You can designate an action to execute if the student clicks in the rollover area rather than rolling over it.

Shortcut: You can type in a keyboard command to run the **On Click** action you designated. If there is no **On Click** action, then the keystroke does not do anything.

On Rollover: When the student rolls over the rollover area, the slidelet appears. In addition, you can set an additional action to execute upon rollover. For example, you can show an object that is somewhere else on the slide. Please note, however, that the action does not undo when the student rolls off the rollover area.

Slide Timeline

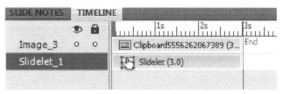

Slidelet Timeline

 # CAUTION

If you use an **On Click** action, be sure to test everything carefully to make sure the actions don't contradict with each other.

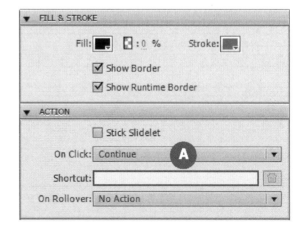

Editing Software Simulations

8

In chapter 2, you learned how to capture software simulation. Your raw captures get you off to a great start when creating your simulations. However, there is usually a fair amount of clean-up to be done. You will often spend more time on editing than you do on the initial capture. That's why it is important to know what your options are and how to work quickly.

In previous chapters, you learned about many features to edit and customize your recordings:

- Add/modify slides, chapter 3
- Add/modify captions and highlight boxes, chapter 4
- Add audio, chapter 5
- Adjust timing of on-screen objects, chapter 6
- Add rollover objects, chapter 7

This chapter shows you features that are specifically designed to help you edit your captures:

- Add/modify mouse movements
- Add/modify typing
- Make changes to the underlying captures
- Edit a full-motion recording clip
- Recapture additional screen shots
- Manage click box slides and text entry slides for interactive practices

Notes

The Editing Process

Once you have your "raw" capture, it is time to edit it. You might need to:

- Correct errors, such as multiple captures or missing captures.
- Refine placement of automatic elements, such as the exact position of a mouse click.
- Add instructional elements, such as an extra caption.
- Modify individual images, such as hiding sensitive information or changing the name of a button.
- Recapture new screen shots.

 CAUTION

Always save your raw capture before making edits. That way, you can go back to your original if you make mistakes during the editing process.

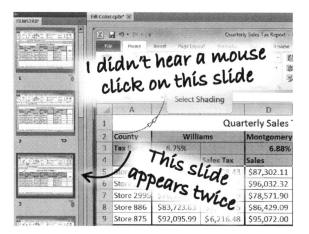

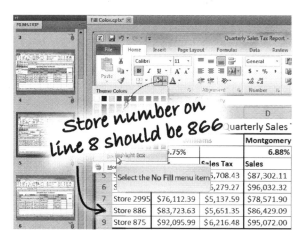

Editing Typing

When you type during a capture, Captivate captures the keystrokes and plays them back one character at a time in the published movie. If you make a mistake in the typing, it is often easier to re-do the slide while capturing. However, sometimes you don't realize you need to make a change until much later, and recapturing the typing again would be too difficult. Fortunately, you are able to go in and edit the typing by converting the typing into a text animation.

Edit Typing

To edit typing:

1. Right-click the typing item in the **Timeline**.
2. Select **Replace with Text Animation**. **(A)**
3. In the **Properties** panel, click the **Properties** button. **(B)**
4. In the **Text** field **(C)**, make text edits to the typing.
5. Click **OK**.

 Text Animations, p. 62

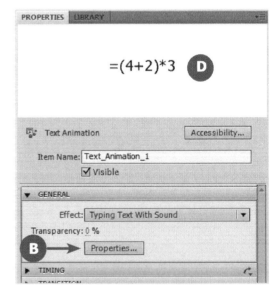

 CAUTION

- Converting the typing to a text animation may change how the characters look. You may need to adjust the formatting or placement of the typing on the screen to make it match.

- Changing the typing on one screen does not change later slides, so you may need to do photo editing on the background later slides. For example, if you changed Excel formula **(D)** to formula **(C)**, the following screens will need to show the answer **2** instead of **18**.

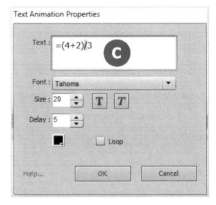

Mouse Movements

When you capture a procedure, you have the option to include the mouse movements. Captivate keeps track of where you click the mouse on each screen and then creates an animated path from point to point on each slide.

Because the mouse movement is "layered" on top of the slides, it is easy to make changes to the movement. For example, you can adjust where the mouse click occurs and what the cursor looks like.

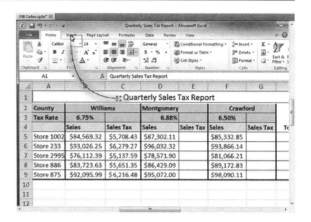

Move the Mouse Click Position

You may need to adjust where the mouse is positioned when it clicks. For example, you may have clicked a menu item in the empty space on the right of that item, which seemed natural during the capture. However, when you review the movie, it seems odd to click off to the side.

To move the mouse click position:

1. Click and drag the mouse cursor to the location you want.

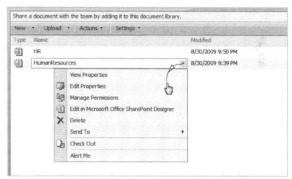

Mouse position from original capture

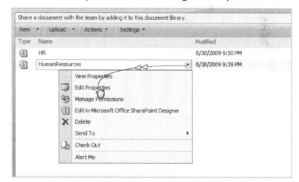

Mouse position after manual adjustment

Change Initial Mouse Position

On each slide, mouse movements start from where they left off on the previous slide. However, on the first slide, there is no such point of reference. Instead, the mouse starts in the upper-left corner. In many cases, this works just fine. However, if your first click is very close to the upper-left corner, your students might not see the mouse move. In cases like this, you might want to change the initial mouse position.

To change the initial mouse position:

1. Click and drag the four red dots to the location you want.

First slide with default starting position

First slide with adjusted starting position

Align Mouse Paths

Because the mouse movement on a slide picks up where the previous slide left off, you should get smooth, fluid movement. However, if you have a slide where you don't want the mouse to move at all, there still might be a little jump in movement because the mouse is not in exactly the same place as it is in the previous slide. You can fix this by aligning the mouse to the previous slide or the next slide.

To align mouse paths with another slide:

1. Right-click the mouse cursor on the slide where you don't want the mouse to move.

2. Select **Align to Previous Slide** or **Align to Next Slide**.

Hide/Show Mouse Movement

Based on how you have your recording settings configured, Captivate automatically includes the mouse movements. However, you may want to hide the movement on certain screens. If you didn't choose to include the mouse when you initially captured, Captivate still "knows" where you clicked on each slide. This means you can add the mouse movement back to any slide during editing.

To hide the mouse movement on a slide:

1. Right-click the mouse cursor on the slide or click the mouse icon under the thumbnail.

2. Deselect **Show Mouse**.

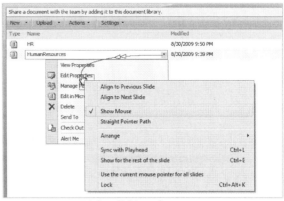

Right-clicking the mouse

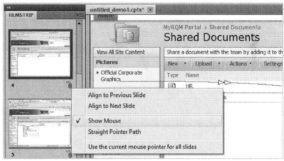

*Right-clicking the mouse icon in the **Filmstrip***

To show the mouse movement on a slide:

1. Right-click the slide or the thumbnail.

2. Select **Mouse**.

3. Select **Show Mouse**.

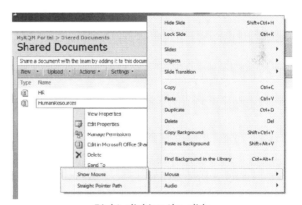

Right-clicking the slide

 **TIME SAVERS**

You can show the mouse by clicking the **Insert Mouse** button on the **Object** toolbar.

You can hide the mouse for the entire project in the **Publish Settings** section of **Preferences**.

 Publish Settings, p. 204

Change Mouse Properties

When you select the mouse cursor on a slide, the **Mouse Properties** pane appears, giving you additional options for how the mouse behaves.

Cursor Type

Captivate adjusts the look of the cursor based on what it looks like in the software. For example, you might see an arrow when clicking a button or an "i-beam" when editing text. You can change the look of the mouse if you need something different.

You can select one of the mouse options shown in the gallery or click the **Browse** button to select from any cursor type included with your operating system.

Double Mouse Size

If you'd like to give the mouse more emphasis, check this box so the mouse appears larger than normal.

Straight Pointer Path

By default, the path of the mouse curves slightly. If you would prefer that it be straight, check this box.

Reduce Speed Before Click

If you check this box, the mouse slows down before the click, which may make the movements appear less abrupt and easier for your students to absorb.

Mouse Click Sound

By default, a click sound is played for every click in the published movie. If you want to change that setting for a given slide, check or uncheck the box.

In addition you can select the sound used for the click. From the drop-down menu, you can select a single-click sound or a double-click sound. You can also click the **Browse** button to select your own sound. The **Play** button lets you hear the selection.

Show Mouse Click

By default, a small blue glow appears with every click in the published movie. If you want to change it for a given slide, check or uncheck the box. In addition, you can click the color picker to change the color of the glow or select **Custom** from the menu to pick from several other options or browse for your own **SWF** file.

Timing

The **Timing** pane lets you adjust when the mouse moves. This can also be done on the **Timeline**.

 Timing Slide Objects, p. 105

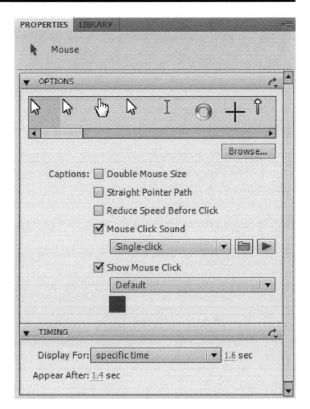

 CAUTION

Don't confuse **Show Mouse** with **Show Mouse Click**. **Show Mouse** determines whether the mouse cursor and movement appear. **Show Mouse Click** determines whether or not there is a glow or other effect associated with the click.

 POWER TIP

In addition to the cursor options shown and those available with your operating system, you can use any CUR file for Windows or PICT file for Mac.

Editing Full-Motion Recording

During a capture, certain actions such as a dragging action trigger a full-motion recording (FMR). You can also manually start FMR in a capture. On screens with FMR, the on-screen action is not presented as an image with the mouse layered on top, but as a video clip in SWF format. On FMR screens, the **Properties** panel has an **FMR Edit Options** pane which lets you:

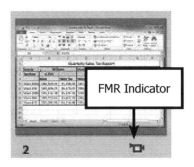

FMR Indicator

- Insert another SWF file.

- Split the FMR into two slides. This is useful if you want to stop in the middle of the video and discuss what has happened.

- Trim the video. This can be helpful when you have "dead" time at the beginning or the end of the FMR.

Recording Settings, p. 21

Edit FMR

To insert another SWF file onto the slide: (A)

1. Click the **Options** drop-down menu.
2. Select **Insert**.
3. Indicate the point when you want to add the clip:
   - Enter the time in the **Insert At** field.
   - Drag the black time marker to the time.
   - Click the **Snap to Playhead** button.
4. Click the **Insert** button.
5. Find and select the **SWF** file you want to insert.
6. Click the **OK** button.

To split the FMR file into two slides: (B)

1. Click the **Options** drop-down menu.
2. Select **Split**.
3. Indicate the point when you want to split the clip:
   - Enter the time in the **Split At** field.
   - Drag the black time marker to the time.
   - Click the **Snap to Playhead** button.
4. Click the **Split** button.

To trim the front and/or end from a clip: (C)

1. Click the **Options** drop-down menu.
2. Select **Trim**.
3. Enter the times you want to start and end the clip:
   - Enter the start and end points in the **Trim From** and **To** fields.
   - Drag each of the two black markers to indicate the start and end points.
   - Click the **Snap to Playhead** button for the start or end point.
4. Click the **Trim** button.

Time Marker | Playhead

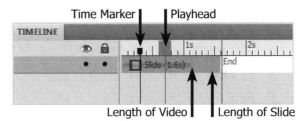

Length of Video | Length of Slide

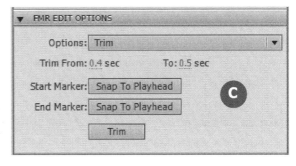

Editing Slide Backgrounds

Each capture in your software simulation is saved as an image. This makes it fairly easy to make changes to those images either using photo editing software or the tools that come with Captivate. For example, you may be creating training for a new software rollout, and at the last minute, the developers change the name of one of the buttons. Instead of redoing the entire capture, you can make background edits to your slides.

Copy and Paste Backgrounds

You can copy the background image of any slide to either paste into another slide or to edit in photo editing software.

To copy a slide background:
1. Right-click the slide.
2. Select **Copy Background**.

To paste an image as a slide background:
1. Copy the image you want to use.
2. Right-click the slide.
3. Select **Paste as Background**.

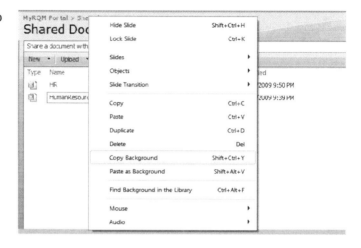

 CAUTION

Be careful about using **Paste** instead of **Paste as Background**. When you use **Paste as Background**, the existing background is replaced with the new image. If you use **Paste**, the new background appears as its own item in the **Timeline** on top of the old background. This adds some risk, because that object could be deleted or moved in the **Timeline**, causing the original background to show.

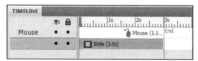

*New background using **Paste as Background***

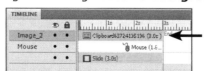

*New background using **Paste***

 POWER TIPS

If you ever need to go back to your original background image, you can find it in the **Library**.

You can save time with photo editing by launching your photo editing software from the **Library**. Right-click the background image you want and select **Edit with**. Then navigate to your photo editing software. This lets you make edits without having to go through the copy and paste steps.

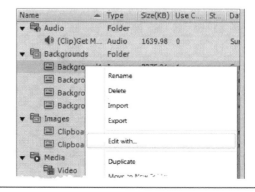

Merge With Background

In addition to using photo editing software to modify your backgrounds and then pasting them back into your capture, you can also use many of the object tools in Captivate to make simple changes. When you use a rectangle, text box, or small image to modify a section of the screen, you'll usually want to merge that image with the background.

Merging with the background combines the existing background and the new object being merged. This keeps the object from being deleted or moved.

To merge an item into the background.

1. Paste or create the object on the slide.
2. Right-click the object.
3. Select **Merge with the background**.

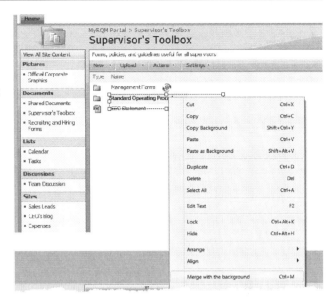

CAUTION

If your new objects are even a pixel off, your students may notice the "jump" when they are viewing your movie. Check your fixes carefully by going back and forth between the previous and next slides or toggle the visibility icon for that object before merging to make sure the fix isn't noticeable.

Use **Merge with the background** when you have an object to add to the background. Use **Paste as Background** when you want to replace the background.

Text caption pasted and merged into background

Text caption pasted as background

DESIGN TIP

Here are some helpful hints about how to use objects to edit your backgrounds.

Shapes

Use the shape tools (rectangle, line, etc.) to cover over solid color areas. This is a great way to cover over a tooltip, a feature that shouldn't be showing, or text that you'll be replacing. Use the eye dropper tool to match the background completely.

Captions

Use a transparent caption to replace text. Change sensitive information such as a customer name, update the name of a feature that has changed, or fix a typo on a non-typing slide.

Sections of Other Slides

Use a screen capture tool such as TechSmith's Jing to capture a small part of another slide to reuse. For example, if an **Enter** button was renamed **OK**, and you have another slide with a similar **OK** button, capture just the area with the **OK** button and paste it on the slide you need to fix.

Recording Additional Slides

After your initial capture, you may need to return to your software application and get additional captures. For example, you may have found an error that can't be fixed by photo-editing the background, or you may have missed a few steps. You can record new slides inside an existing capture.

Record Additional Slides

To record additional slides:

1. Click the **Record additional slides for this project** button on the **Main Options** toolbar.

2. Select the slide after which the recorded slides should be inserted.

3. Click the **OK** button.

4. Configure your capture settings.

5. Click the **Record** button.

6. Capture your screens as you did before.

7. Press the **End** key on your keyboard.

Instead of clicking the **Record** button shown above, you can also go to the **Insert** menu, and select **Recording Slides**.

 Record a Software Simulation, p. 20

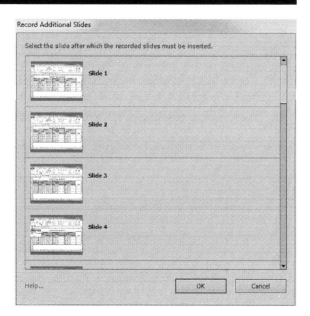

 TIME SAVERS

- Set up everything for the new slides before you click **Record**. For example, you may need to undo some of the steps you performed in the original capture, especially if the new slides go in the middle of the project. For example, if you approved a vacation request at the end of a project, you may need to "unapprove" it before you can recapture an earlier step.

- Use the **Snap to window** feature during the initial recording and any additional recording to reduce the chance of your new captures being misaligned with your original captures.

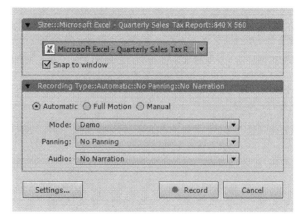

 CAUTION

Not all of the recording options are available when you are adding additional captures. For example, the size of the recording window is locked to the size of the existing project.

Managing Practice Slides

When you create an interactive practice (such as training or assessment mode), Captivate adds either click boxes or text entry boxes to create the student interactivity. You can manage the properties of the click boxes and text entry boxes, and you can also add your own if you want to.

Here are some special considerations when dealing with practice slides: click boxes and text entry boxes.

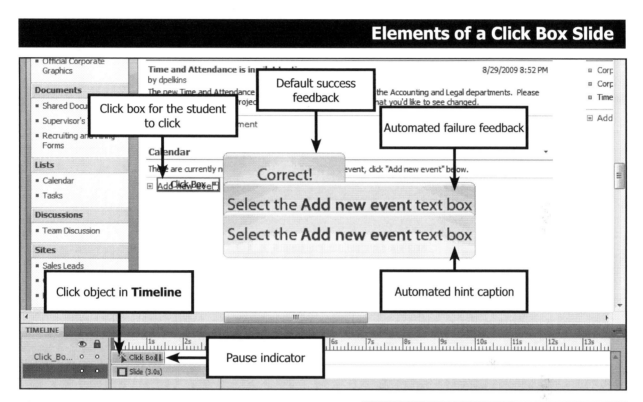

Elements of a Click Box Slide

Placement: Be sure that the click box fully covers the area that the student should click. In some cases, the default placement only covers half of the button, menu item, etc. Click and drag the click box to move or resize it.

Action Pane: By default, students go to the next slide when they click correctly, and the slide continues if they do not click correctly in the designated number of attempts. This means the rest of the slide plays, so you can put an extra caption with feedback after the pause indicator. Only the students who don't click in the set number of attempts will ever see that caption.

You can also designate a keyboard shortcut to take the place of a click.

Options Pane: Here you can change many of the options you selected in the **Recording Settings**. In addition, you can change a left-click to a double-click or right-click.

Click Box Properties, p. 114

Elements of a Text Entry Box Slide

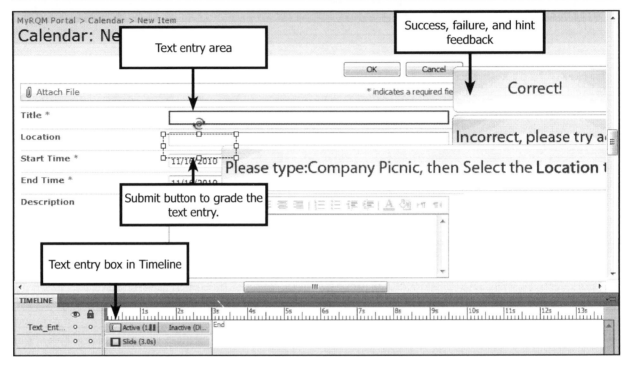

MyRQM Portal > Calendar > New Item

Calendar: Ne

Text entry area

Success, failure, and hint feedback

OK   Cancel

📎 Attach File   * indicates a required fie

Correct!

Title *

Location

Incorrect, please try a

Start Time *   11/18/2010

Please type:Company Picnic, then Select the **Location**

End Time *   11/18/2010

Description   Submit button to grade the text entry.

Text entry box in Timeline

TIMELINE

Text_Ent...   Active (1.⬛⬛)   Inactive (Di... End
              Slide (3.0s)

Placement: You may need to adjust the formatting or size of the text entry box to match everything else on the screen.

Grading the Answer: When a student types in an answer, Captivate needs to know when to grade it.

- **Keyboard Shortcut**: If you enter a shortcut **(A)**, the students' entries are graded when they press that shortcut.

- **Submit Button**: If you check **Show Button (B)**, a **Submit** button appears next to the text box (sometimes hidden under a caption). The student's answer is graded when he or she clicks the **Submit** button.

- **Combine the Submit Button With the Next Step**: If the next step in the procedure is a click, use the **Submit** button, but make it transparent and place it over the step. That way, when the student clicks the next step (such as clicking the **OK** button), the text entry will be graded.

 CAUTION

With the first two options, the student performs a step that is not part of the procedure. The student might get used to pressing **Enter** or clicking **Submit**, and then try to do it in the real system. The third option avoids this. In all cases, include clear instructions about what the student should do.

 Text Entry Box Properties, p. 118

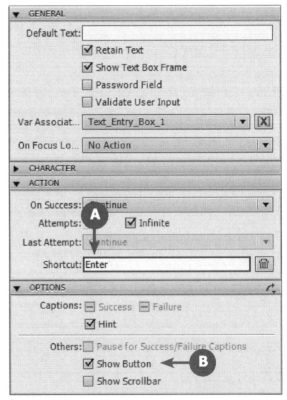

GENERAL

Default Text:

☑ Retain Text
☑ Show Text Box Frame
☐ Password Field
☐ Validate User Input

Var Associat...   Text_Entry_Box_1   ▼   [X]

On Focus Lo...   No Action   ▼

CHARACTER

ACTION

On Success: ntinue   ▼
Attempts: ☑ Infinite
Last Attempt: ntinue   ▼
Shortcut: Enter   🗑

OPTIONS

Captions: ☐ Success ☐ Failure
☑ Hint

Others: ☐ Pause for Success/Failure Captions
☑ Show Button ◀ B
☐ Show Scrollbar

Variables & Advanced Actions

9

Variables and advanced actions let you expand and customize the functionality of Captivate. They are like building blocks that you can use however you want to create special features.

A variable is a stored piece of logic within the project that you can use to:

- Track information provided by the student, such as an option that the student selects or text that the student enters.

- Control course functionality, such as turning the audio or the control playbar on and off.

- Display something back to the student, such as the current time or points earned in a test or game.

- Set up conditional logic, such as whether or not a student is a supervisor or uses a screen reader.

Advanced actions give you more choices than you have in the **Actions** pane of an object's properties. Use the **Advanced Actions** dialog box when you want to:

- Apply more than one action to a single object. For example, in a game, you might want a single button click to show a message, add points to a score, and advance to the next slide.

- Create a conditional action. For example, you can ask students if they are a supervisor or not, and then have a button that branches to one slide if they click **Yes** and a different slide if they click **No**.

- Reuse actions. For example, if you want to add points to a student's score in a game that has several questions, you can set up the action once and then reuse it on each slide.

- Access more action options. For example, you can create calculations from the **Advanced Actions** dialog box.

- Interact with objects on different slides. For example, you can have a button on slide 3 that reveals an object on slide 10.

Notes

Working With Variables

Variables, which are stored pieces of information in the project, come in two basic types.

- **System Variables**: System variables are set up by Captivate. They include information about the project (such as the current slide), controls for the project (such as whether the playbar is showing), or quiz information, if there is a quiz. You cannot set up or delete these variables, but you can use them for conditional logic, display them to students, and even modify some of them to control the project.

   Appendix: System Variables, p. 225

- **User Variables**: A user variable is one that you create yourself. You set it up, you define and modify its value, and you decide how it will be used. For example, you can set up a variable to keep score in a game. You can also set up variables that the student controls. For example, you can enter a text box where the student enters his or her name, and then you use that information later in a certificate.

Manage Variables

To manage variables:

1. Go to the **Project** menu.
2. Select **Variables**.
3. Select **User** or **System** from the **Type** menu to see a list of each type of variable.

System variables can only be viewed, not modified, in this dialog box. Select one from the list to view its current value and the description.

For user variables, you can delete or change the default value of the variable.

To delete a user variable:

1. Select a variable.
2. Click the **Remove** button.

To change the default value of a user variable:

1. Select a variable.
2. Change the value (or description).
3. Click the **Update** button.

Add a User Variable

To add a user variable:

1. Go to the **Project** menu.
2. Select **Variables**.
3. Click the **Add New** button.
4. In the **Name** field, enter the name for the variable.
5. In the **Value** field, enter the initial value for the variable.
6. In the **Description** field, add a description about the variable or how it will be used, if needed.
7. Click the **Save** button.
8. Click the **Close** button.

Variable names cannot contain spaces or special characters except underscore.

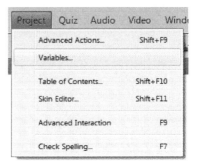

 TIME SAVER

Put an underscore in front of the name of your variables so they'll be easier to find at the top of the variable lists.

Add a Student-Entry Variable

When you add a text entry field to a project, the student's entry is saved as a variable. You can then use this for conditional logic or to display back to the student. For example, you may have the student enter his or her name.

In the **General** pane for the text entry box, use the **Var Associated** field to indicate what variable you want to use to capture the student's answer. Either select an existing variable from the drop-down menu or click the **X** button to create a new variable for it.

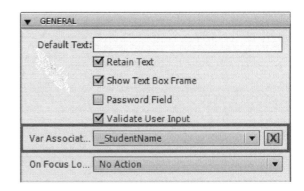

 Text Entry Boxes, p. 118

Modify Variables With the Actions Pane

Variables can be modified with simple actions from the **Action** pane of the various trigger objects. More advanced modifications can be done with advanced actions.

Assign

Use this command to change the value of a variable to an exact value, such as a number or text. For example, you might want to turn off the playbar on a given slide or pause the project when a student clicks a button.

Increment

Use this command to add to a user-defined variable that has a number value. For example, you can add points to a student's score in a game.

Decrement

Use this command to subtract from a variable that has a number value. For example, you can subtract points from a student's score.

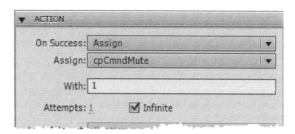

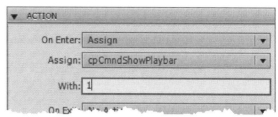

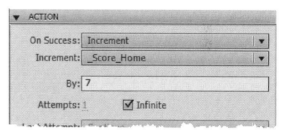

Display a Variable

You can display the value of a variable to the student in a text caption or a shape with text. The variable can be included with other text. The text is updated every time the variable is updated.

For example, you might want to display the student's point value during a game or display an answer that the student previously entered in a text box.

To display a variable:

1. Double-click a caption or shape with text.
2. Click the **Insert Variables** button. **(A)**
3. Select the **User** or **System** from the **Variable Type** menu, based on the type of variable you want to display.
4. In the **Variables** field, select the variable you want.
5. Click the **OK** button.

Click the **Variables** button if you want to go to the **Variables** dialog box to add or make changes to the variables.

The **Maximum length** field shows the maximum number of characters that will be displayed. If the value of the variable is longer than that, the extra characters will be cut off.

 POWER TIP

If you prefer, you can type the variable code into the caption yourself. Type two dollar signs before and after the name of the variable. The variable must be an exact match, including capitalization.

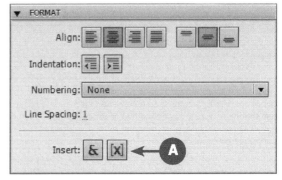

Variable placeholder in edit mode.

Variable placeholder in published movie.

Advanced Actions

Remember that the **Advanced Actions** dialog box gives you more options than you get from the **Actions** pane in an object's properties, such as grouping actions together or creating conditional actions.

When you create an advanced action, it becomes available for use anywhere in the project. But it does not run on its own. Therefore, you must create an action that runs the advanced action. For example, if you create an advanced action that runs the logic when a student scores points in a game, you still need to create an action that runs the logic.

1. **Create the Action** → 2. **Execute the Action**

Execute Advanced Actions, p. 110

Add a Standard Advanced Action

To add a standard action:

1. Go to the **Project** menu.
2. Select **Advanced Actions**.
3. In the **Action Name** field, enter a name for the action.
4. In the **Actions** list, double-click in the second column.
5. Select the action you want from the drop-down arrow.
6. Complete the additional options that may appear in the third column, based on the action you chose.
7. Repeat steps 4-6 for additional commands in the same action.
8. Click the **Save** button.
9. Click the **Close** button.

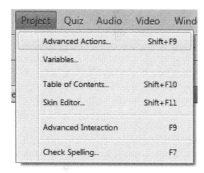

Special Options

- Colored icons indicate if the action is complete. A green icon means the action is complete. A red icon means there is missing or incomplete information. You cannot save an advanced action with a red icon.

- Click the **Variables** button to add or change variables.

- Use the icons just above the **Actions** list to modify individual actions.

  Add: Add a new row at the bottom. This does the same thing as double-clicking in the next available row.

  Remove: Delete the selected individual action.

  Cut, **Copy**, and **Paste**: Use to make copies of an individual action.

  Insert: Add a line above the selected action.

  Move Up and **Move Down**: Change the order of the selected action.

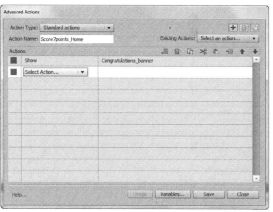

Advanced Action Types

Many of the action types available in the **Advanced Action** dialog box are the same as what is available in the **Action** pane. However, some of them are set up differently in this dialog box, and there are additional actions available as well.

The following actions work the same way in the **Actions** pane and the **Advanced Actions** dialog box:

- Continue
- Go to Next Slide
- Go to Previous Slide
- Go to Last Visited Slide
- Jump to Slide
- Open URL/File
- Open Another Project
- Send Mail
- Execute JavaScript
- Apply Effect

The following actions are slightly different with advanced actions:

Enable, Disable, Show, and Hide

These work *mostly* the same way as they do in the **Actions** pane. In the **Actions** pane, you can only select items on that slide. In the **Advanced Actions** dialog box, you can select any eligible object in the project.

Assign

The **Assign** action still lets you assign a valuable to a variable. However, you have some additional choices.

Once you select **Assign** from the action column, you can then select the variable you want from the drop-down menu from the second column.

Next, a new menu appears letting you choose **literal** or **variable**.

- Select **literal** if you want to use an exact value, such as a number or text.
- Select **variable** if you want to change the value of the first **variable** to the value of a second variable.

The **Expression** action is only available for advanced actions. **Expression** lets you create calculations, taking the place of and providing more options than **Increment** and **Decrement**.

First, select a variable that will hold the value of the calculation.

You can make either part of the equation a variable or either part a literal value. First select **variable** or **literal** from the menu. If you select **variable**, you get a list of variables to choose from. If you select **literal**, you get a text entry box to enter the literal value.

Finally, you can select from four calculation types: addition, subtraction, multiplication, or division.

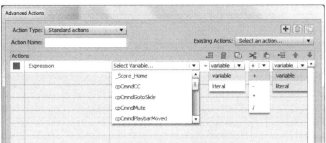

Options for building the expression

Finished expression

Conditional Actions

With a standard advanced action, all actions run when the advanced action is executed. When a conditional action is executed, the actions only run if certain conditions are met. For example, certain information might be shown if the quiz is passed. A conditional action can have three parts.

- **If**: This is where you set up the conditions that have to be met in order for the actions to run.
- **Actions**: This is where you set up the individual actions that will run when the conditions are met.
- **Else**: Here you can set up an alternate set of actions that will run if the conditions are NOT met. You can leave this section blank, which means that nothing will happen if the conditions are not met.

As with standard advanced actions, you need to first set up the advanced action, and then execute it from the **Action** pane of an interactive object.

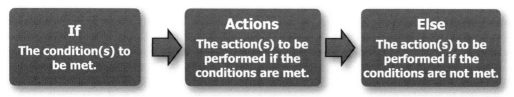

Add a Conditional Advanced Action

To add a conditional action:

1. Go to the **Project** menu.
2. Select **Advanced Actions**.
3. From the **Action Type** menu, select **Conditional actions**.
4. In the **Action Name** field, enter a name for the action.
5. In the **IF** section, enter the condition(s) that need to occur in order for the action to run.
6. In the **Actions** section, enter the action(s) that will run when the **IF** conditions are met.
7. Click the **ELSE** heading.
8. Enter the action(s) that will run if the **IF** conditions are not met.
9. Click the **Save** button.
10. Click the **Close** button.

Refer to the next few pages for details on the **IF**, **Actions**, and **ELSE** sections.

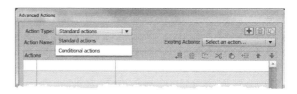

Creating IF Conditions

A condition has three parts: the two items being compared and how they should be compared. Double-click a line in the **IF** section, and enter values for the three parts.

1. Select a variable or literal value for the basis of comparison.

2. Select a comparison operator to determine how the two items will be compared.

   - **Is greater than**
   - **Is less than**
   - **Greater or equal to**
   - **Lesser or equal to**
   - **Not equal to**
   - **Is equal to**
   - **Contains**

3. Select what the first value should be compared to, either another variable or a literal value.

Options for building the conditions

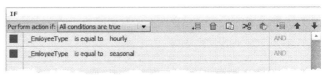

Finished condition

Multiple Conditions

You can create an advanced action with one or more conditions. If there is only one condition, then you don't need to do anything more. However, if you have multiple conditions, you need to designate how the conditions interact with each other.

From the **Perform action if** drop-down menu, select one of the following:

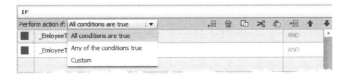

All Conditions Are True: Select this option if all conditions must be met in order for the actions to be run. This is the same as AND logic.

Any of the Conditions Are True: Select this option if you only need one of the options to be true for the actions to be run. This is the same as OR logic.

Custom: Select this option if you want to use a combination of AND and OR logic. When you use this option, select **AND** or **OR** for each condition in the third column.

Managing Conditions

Conditions can be copied, pasted, moved, etc. just as actions can.

Creating Actions and Else Actions

In the **Actions** section, add one or more action just as with standard actions.

To set up else actions, click the **ELSE** heading. Then add the actions just as with standard actions.

Click the **IF** heading to return to the original view.

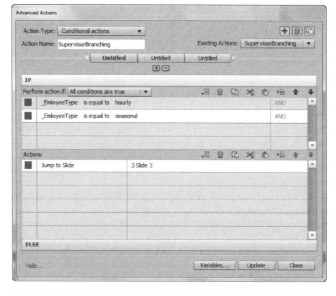

Creating Multiple Decisions

Just as a standard action can have multiple individual actions, a conditional action can have multiple decisions, meaning multiple if/action/else sets. For example, the advanced action runs one set of logic based on the employee type and a second set of logic based on whether the test was passed. Decisions are managed by the buttons in the middle of the dialog box.

- To view a decision, click the button for that decision.

- To rename a decision, double-click the button for that decision, and type the name.

- To add a new decision, click the **Plus** button.

- To delete a decision, click the button for the decision and then click the **Minus** button.

Managing Advanced Actions

From the **Advanced Actions** dialog box, you can manage existing actions.

- To view an advanced action, select it from the **Existing Actions** drop-down menu.

- To add an additional advanced action, click the **Create a new action** button.

- To delete an advanced action, select it, and then click the **Delete action** button.

- To make a copy of an advanced action, select it, and then click the **Duplicate action** button.

- To modify an advanced action (rename it or add or delete actions and conditions), make the changes, and click the **Update** button.

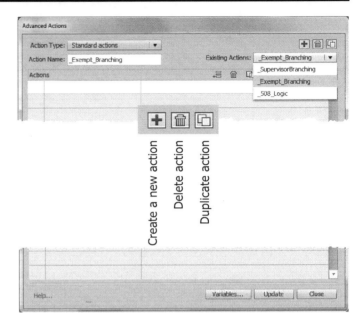

Create a new action

Delete action

Duplicate action

CAUTION

When you are working with more than one action, make sure they are in the proper order. Actions are executed in order from top to bottom. For example, if you are showing an object and then going to the next page, be sure to put them in that order. Otherwise, the student will go to the next page before the object appears.

Advanced Interactions Panel

The **Advanced Interactions** panel lets you see all the interactive objects in your project. From this one view, you can see many of the key properties of the interactive objects, such as the action, number of attempts, etc. When you click on an object in the pane, the slide appears with the object selected and the object's **Properties** panel showing.

You can access the **Advanced Interactions** panel from the **Project** menu.

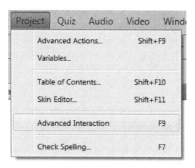

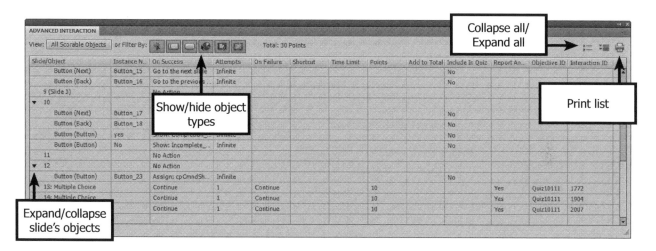

Collapse all/ Expand all

Print list

Show/hide object types

Expand/collapse slide's objects

Notes

Questions & Quizzes 10

Questions, quizzes, tests, scenarios, interactions—these course elements often make the difference between telling someone something and teaching them something. They allow both you and the students to reinforce and apply the content, assess the learning, uncover opportunities for re-teaching, and evaluate the course effectiveness. Captivate offers nine question types you can insert in a graded format and/or survey format.

In this chapter you will learn how to add questions to your projects either for pure reinforcement or as part of a graded quiz that reports to a learning management system (LMS). (You'll learn more about the LMS reporting settings in chapter 12.)

In this chapter:
- Adding Questions
- Configuring Questions
- Question Pools
- Quiz Templates
- Quiz Results
- Quiz Preferences

Notes

Add a Question

To add a question to your project:

1. Go to the **Insert** or **Quiz** menu.
2. Select **Question Slide**.
3. Check the box for the type of question you would like to use.
4. Enter the quantity you want for that question type.
5. Select **Graded** or **Survey** from the drop-down menu.
6. Click **OK**.

 TIME SAVER

You can add several questions at once in this dialog box by selecting more than one type of question and entering the quantity you want for each before clicking **OK**.

 POWER TIP

You can also include custom interactive objects in your quizzes. For example, you can track whether a student clicks a button you added to a regular slide or clicks a click box in a practice simulation. Just check the **Include in Quiz** check box in the **Reporting** pane for that object.

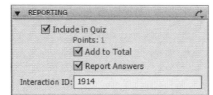

 Click Boxes and Buttons, pp. 114-116

 DESIGN TIP

Graded vs. Survey Questions

Use a graded question type when there are right and wrong answers. You can indicate which answer is right vs. wrong and provide separate feedback for each question. Most knowledge-check questions fall into this category.

Use a survey question when there isn't a right or wrong answer. You cannot designate a right or wrong answer, and all students get the same feedback, regardless of their answer. This is most often used for opinion-style questions or questions where the student self-grades their answer as compared to the answer you provide.

Question Types

Multiple Choice	
Student chooses one or more options among several possible answers. • Can have up to 15 answer choices • Available as graded or survey	**When dealing with an angry customer, it is best to:** ○ A) maintain a calm, soothing voice ◉ B) mirror the client's energy to let him or her know you understand the frustration ○ C) speak to the customer firmly telling him or her to calm down ○ D) ask the customer to take a few minutes to relax
True/False Student decides between two options. • Can change "true" and "false" labels • Available as graded or survey	**As an organization, we believe there are opportunities to learn from clients willing to share their complaints.** ◉ A) True ○ B) False
Fill in the Blank Student types a word into the space provided. • Can be case sensitive or not • Can have more than one possible answer • Can be formatted as a multiple-choice question with a drop-down list • Available as graded or survey	**Complete the sentence below by filling in the blank.** The first thing we must do with an angry customer is _____ him or her. **Complete the sentence below by filling in the blank.** The first thing we must do with an angry customer is [▼] him or her. move listen to calm
Short Answer Student types in a longer answer to a question. • Available as graded or survey	**What do you believe are the two or three most important qualities a customer service specialist possesses?** ⸴

Question Types

Matching

Student matches items in one column with items in the other.

- Can have up to 8 options per column
- Available as graded or survey

Column 1		Column 2
C	Shannon Fielding	A) VP of Customer Care
A	Jackson Roberts	B) Legal Counsel
B	Maria Velasquez	C) Senior Manager - Customer Care

Hot Spot

Student clicks on one or more designated hot spots on a graphic image.

- Can have up to 10 hot spots
- Available as graded or survey

Where is our largest customer base? Choose the correct city from the list of hotspots.

Sequence

Student arranges a series of items into the proper sequence.

- Can be formatted as a drag-and-drop or drop-down list
- Available as graded or survey

Arrange in sequence

A) Customer is connected to a Customer Care Associate.

B) Customer calls the Customer Care Hotline.

C) Customer is upset and decides to complain.

D) Issue is not resolved via the computerized system.

Arrange in sequence

A) Customer is upset and decides to complain. ▼

B) Customer calls the Customer Care Hotline. ▼

C) --Select-- ▼

D) Customer calls the Customer Care Hotline.

Customer is upset and decides to complain.

Customer is connected to a Customer Care Associate.

Issue is not resolved via the computerized system.

Rating Scale (Likert)

Students evaluate statements and rate them on a scale.

- Can have up to 5 points on the scale
- Available as survey only

Indicate how strongly you agree or disagree with the following:

	Disagree 1	Somewhat Disagree 2	Neutral 3	Somewhat Agree 4	Agree 5
A) I feel empowered to meet the customers' needs.	○	○	○	○	○
B) I feel competent to handle most customer complaints.	○	○	○	○	○

Configuring Questions

Once you've added your question, you'll need to configure it, changing both the text and the properties. Some options are changed directly on the slide and some are changed on the **Quiz Properties** tab.

The options vary based on question type. The next four pages cover standard properties and options that apply to most questions types. The following pages go into question type-specific options.

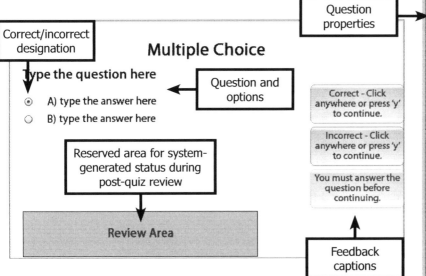
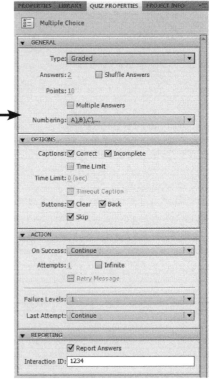

Add Question Content

Your question slide has placeholders for a title, your question/instructions, and the answer options. To build your question, simply type or paste your text into the appropriate placeholders.

To format the text boxes:

1. Select the object(s) you want to format.
2. Click the **Properties** tab.
3. Make the changes you want.

To add more answer options (except T/F):

1. Click the **Quiz Properties** tab.
2. Enter the number you want in the **Answers** field.

 CAUTION

Don't get confused by the **Properties** and **Quiz Properties** tabs. Use the **Properties** tab for object options such as font or color. Use **Quiz Properties** for question-specific options such as the number of correct answers or what feedback options to include.

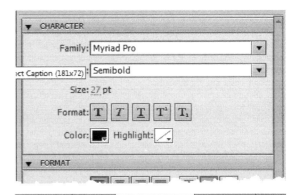

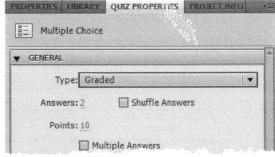

Customize Feedback

You can have up to five types of feedback captions, which can be turned on and off via the **Quiz Properties** tab. Change the text, formatting, and location of the feedback caption just like you would any other caption.

A. Correct: This caption displays when the student answers the question correctly.

> Correct - Click anywhere or press 'y' to continue.

B. Incorrect: This caption displays when the student answers the question incorrectly.

> Incorrect - Click anywhere or press 'y' to continue.

C. Timeout: If you set a time limit for the question, this caption appears when the time runs out.

> The time to answer this question has expired. Click anywhere or press 'y' to continue.

D. Retry: If you allow more than one attempt, this caption appears after each failed attempt (except the last one).

> Try again

E. Required Answer: If the question cannot be skipped, this caption appears if the student tries to leave the page without answering the question.

> You must answer the question before continuing.

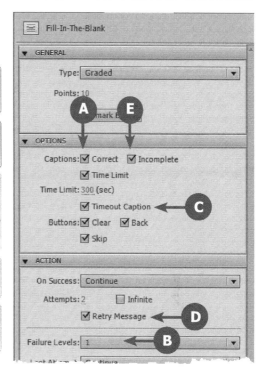

 Caption Properties, p. 50

DESIGN TIPS

- Keep in mind that the student will never see all the captions at once—they only appear based on certain student actions. Because of that, some of your captions can overlap each other. For example, the correct and incorrect captions would never appear at once, so you can overlap them on your slide. However, the timer caption might appear at the same time as another caption, so it should not overlap the others.

- Use the **Time Limit** option with care. Imposing a time limit has accessibility implications for those with physical, cognitive, or developmental disabilities.

- You can use caption styles to help save time with formatting your feedback captions.

   Styles, p. 98

- If you want to provide more feedback than can be included in a single text caption, consider creating a separate slide for the feedback and using the **Action** panel to branch to the appropriate slide.

  Action Pane, p. 159

Quiz Properties

The **Quiz Properties** tab lets you customize your question. Many of the choices are the same for most question types. These are covered here. Some properties are unique to each question type. These are covered in the subsequent pages.

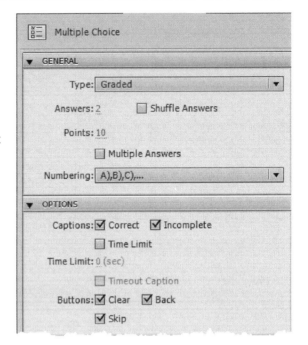

General Pane

Type: Select either **Graded** if you want points, answer validation, and right/wrong feedback, or **Survey** if you want the same feedback regardless of the answer given.

Answers: Enter the number of answer choices you want.

Shuffle Answers: Check this box if you want the program to shuffle the possible answers. This is great if you don't want your students to "share" answers.

Points: Enter a point value (from 1 to 100) for graded questions.

Multiple Answers: Check this box if your question has more than one right answer (e.g., Select all that apply...).

Numbering: Change the type of numbers, letters, and punctuation for the answer options.

Options Pane

Captions: Check the boxes for **Correct** or **Incomplete** if you want to include those captions with the question.

Time Limit: Check this box if you want to sets a time limit for answering the question. If you check the **Time Limit** box, enter the number of seconds you to give the students for answering the question.

Timeout Caption: If you choose to add a time limit, check this box if you want to add a caption that appears when time runs out.

Buttons: These buttons appear at the bottom of the slide giving students options to maneuver through the training. Check or uncheck the boxes based on which buttons you want to include on the slide.

Quiz Properties (continued)

Action Pane

On Success: Click the drop-down menu to select what should happen when students get the answer correct.

Attempts: Select the number of times you will let students try to answer, or check **Infinite** to give them unlimited tries.

Retry Message: If you allow 2 or more attempts to answer, check this box if you want to add a caption that asks the student to try again.

Failure Levels: Use this drop-down menu to indicate how many separate feedback captions you want. That way, you can provide progressively more detailed feedback with each incorrect answer. You can have a maximum of three levels and cannot have more failure levels than you have attempts.

Last Attempt: Indicate the action you want if the student is unable to answer the question correctly after the maximum number of attempts. This option is not available if you select **Infinite** attempts.

 Action Types, p. 109

 DESIGN TIP

Use the **Action** panel to create branching simulations. Use the **Jump to Slide** action for success to branch to one slide if the student gets it right and then jump to a different slide on the last attempt if they get it wrong.

Reporting Pane

Report Answers: If you check this box, question-specific data will be sent to the learning management system, rather than just the overall test score.

Interaction ID: If you are sending question-specific data to the LMS, you can enter an interaction number to be sent to the LMS.

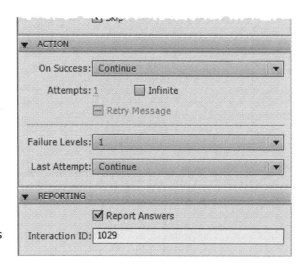

On Success and Last Attempt action options

Review Area

The **Review Area** is a portion of the slide reserved for system-generated feedback when the student goes back and reviews a quiz. You can move and resize the review area to design your page.

From **Quiz Preferences**, you can enable or disable the review area and change the default text for the entire quiz. If you want to change the text used for a specific question, select the review area for that question, and then go to the **Properties** (not the **Quiz Properties**) tab. You can make edits to the text in the **Review Feedback Messages** pane.

 Quiz Preferences p. 172

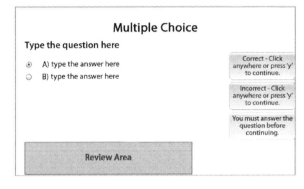

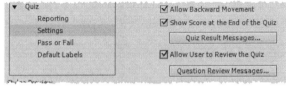

 # CAUTION

Make sure you do not cover up the review area with any of your slide elements.

If you resize the review area, check it in preview mode to make sure there is still enough room for all the text.

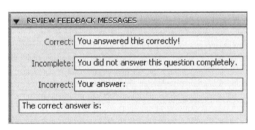

True/False Question Options

True/False questions do not have any additional properties. You can, however, edit the answer text boxes on the slide to change from true/false to yes/no, right/wrong, etc.

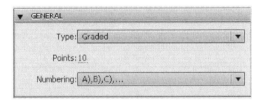

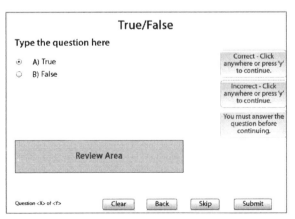

Fill-in-the-Blank Question Options

To set up a fill-in-the-blank question:
1. Type your full statement in the text box provided.
2. Select the word/phrase you want the student to fill in.
3. Click the **Mark Blank** button **(A)**

The part that the student fills in appears underlined in edit mode, but appears as a blank in preview mode.

To enter more than one possible correct answer:
1. Double-click your underlined word or phrase. **(B)**
2. Click the **Plus** button. **(C)**
3. Type an additional correct answer in the box.
4. Repeat steps 2 and 3 for any other answers you want.
5. Click anywhere on the slide to exit the menu.

To convert to a drop-down multiple-choice question:
1. Double-click your underlined word or phrase.
2. Click the **User Input** drop-down menu. **(D)**
3. Select **Dropdown List**.
4. Click the **Plus** button.
5. Type an answer option.
6. Repeat steps 4 and 5 for additional answer options.
7. Check the box(es) next to the correct answer(s). **(E)**
8. Click anywhere on the slide to exit the menu.

BRIGHT IDEAS

- For user input questions, check **Case Sensitive** if you want students to match your capitalization.
- For dropdown list questions, check **Shuffle Answers** if you want to randomize the options.
- Select an option and click **Minus** button to delete an answer you've entered but don't want.
- You can mark more than one blank in a question. Use the drop-down list **(F)** to modify each.

CAUTION

- Be careful about user input questions with many correct answers. For example, if the answer is 12:00 p.m., use a dropdown list because of all the correct ways someone could enter that time.

- You can have multiple correct answers on a dropdown list question. It may not be obvious to the students that they can select more than one answer, so either use very clear instructions, or use the multiple-choice question type.

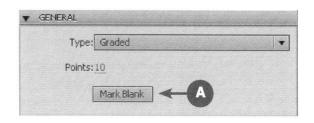

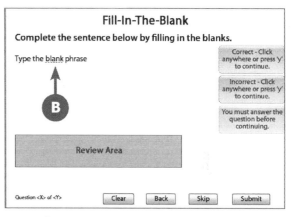

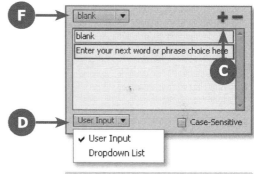

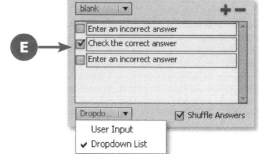

Short Answer Question Options

To enter the correct answer for a graded short answer question:

1. Click the answer text box.
2. Enter the correct answer.
3. Click anywhere on the slide to exit the dialog box.

Options

- Use the **Plus** button to enter more than one acceptable answer.
- Select an answer, and click the **Minus** button to delete that possible answer.
- Check the **Case-Sensitive** box if you want the student to match the capitalization you used.

DESIGN TIPS

- Most short-answer questions are not system-graded because the students are often providing their thoughts and ideas, rather than a specific answer. With a survey question, you can still use a single caption with some feedback, or take them to another slide that gives some possible answers for the students to compare their answers with.

- It is best to use a graded short answer test when there is an exact right answer, rather than something subjective. For example, you could use a graded question for "What is our mission statement?" which has only one correct answer, and use a survey question for "How can you put the customer first?" which can have many ways to express the correct answer.

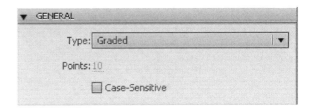

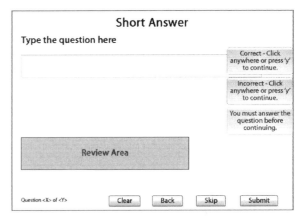

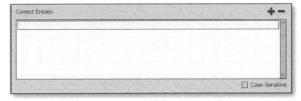

Matching Question Options

To set up a matching question:

1. On the **Quiz Properties** tab, enter the number of options you want in each column.

2. Type your options in the text boxes on the slides.

3. Enter the correct match from column 2 next to each item in column 1.

4. Check **Shuffle Column 1** if you want to Captivate to rearrange column 1 to create a different match pattern each time.

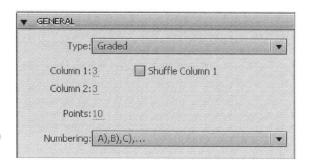

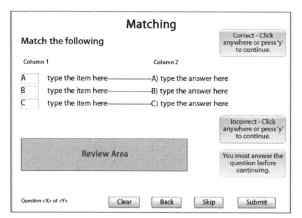

DESIGN TIPS

- If you want to have distractors (items without a match), then have more items in column 2 than column 1.

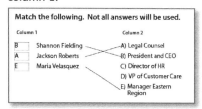

- If you want to have one item match to more than one answer, have more items in column 1 than column 2.

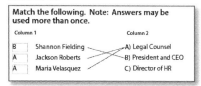

- Be sure to add instructions to let students know about the unmatched or double-matched options.

Hot Spot Question Options

To set up a hot spot question:

1. Place your image on the page.
2. On the **Quiz Properties** tab, enter the number of hot spots you want to include (number of answers).
3. Position the hot spot areas to the appropriate places on your image.
4. Click the **Properties** tab.
5. Select a hot spot.
6. Check or uncheck the **Correct Answer** box.
7. Repeat steps 4-6 for the additional hot spots.

Quiz Properties Options

Hotspot: When students click on the image, a blue star appears to indicate where they clicked. If you want to change the look of that marker, click the **Browse** button, **(A)** and select a different animation.

Default   *Sample options*

Allow Clicks Only on Hotspots: Check this box **(B)** if you don't want to let the student register a click anywhere other than the designated hotspots. Use this if you want to create visible, incorrect hotspots. Keep it unchecked if you only want to create correct, invisible hot spots and have all the rest of the image considered incorrect.

Individual Hot Spot Properties Options

Show Hand Cursor Over Hit Area: Check this box **(C)** if you want the student's cursor to change to a hand when it is over any of the hot spots. This is a clue to let students know it is a hot spot.

Fill & Stroke: You can make the hot spots either visible or invisible, based on whether or not you use a fill and stroke. Keep them invisible for a more challenging question that makes the student consider all parts of the image. Make them visible if you only want the students to consider certain areas of the image, as in the one shown on the right.

 Fill & Stroke, p. 90

 DESIGN TIP

Be sure to provide clear instructions! For example, let students know if more than one hot spot is correct and that they can undo a selection by clicking the same spot again.

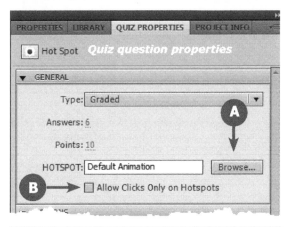

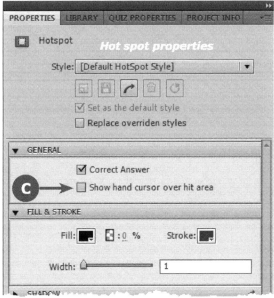

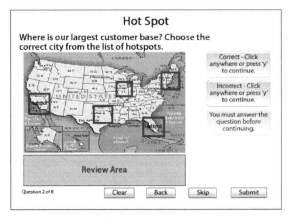

Sequence Question Options

When you set up a sequence question, you enter the items in the proper order, and then Captivate mixes the options up for the student in the published movie.

To set up a sequence question:

1. In the Answers **field**, enter the number of items you want to use.

2. Enter the answer options in the provided text fields in the correct order.

3. In the **Answer Type** field, select either **Drag Drop** or **Drop Down** based on the question format you want.

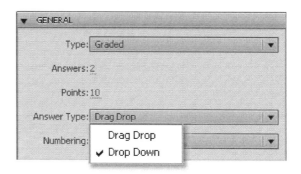

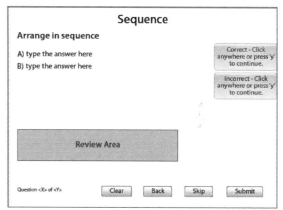

DESIGN TIP

As with all question types, include clear directions. Students may not realize they are supposed to drag the items around or select them from a drop-down list.

Rating Scale (Likert) Question Properties

To set up a rating scale question:

1. In the **Answers** field, enter the number of statements you want the student to evaluate.

2. In the **Rating Scale** field, select the number of options you want on the scale (maximum 5).

3. Enter your evaluation items in the text boxes down the side.

4. Change the rating scale text across the top if you want to use a different scale.

Remember that rating scale questions are only available as survey questions. There are no right or wrong answers, grading, or points.

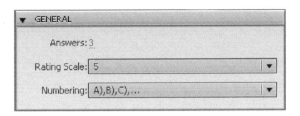

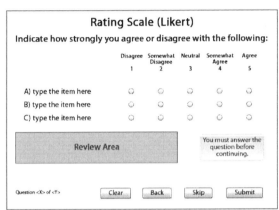

Question Pools

Question pools let you add questions at random to your presentation, making each user's experience unique. Rather than entering a specific question at a certain point in the project, Captivate selects a question from a group (or pool) of questions that you've created on a subject. You can create as many pools as you'd like.

Use question pools when you want to discourage "sharing" of answers or when you want students to get a different set of questions if they need to retry the quiz.

Question pools are separate entities from the actual presentation. If all you do is create a question pool, no questions will appear in your project. You'll need to insert a random question from the pool for them to appear in your project. It's only then that you'll see the question in the filmstrip.

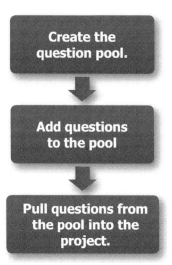

Create the question pool.

Add questions to the pool

Pull questions from the pool into the project.

Create a Question Pool

To create a new question pool:

1. Click the **Quiz** menu.
2. Select **Question Pool Manager**.
3. Type the name for your pool in the box on the left.
4. Click the **Plus** sign in the upper-left corner to create additional pools.
5. Type the name for the additional pools.
6. Click **Close**.

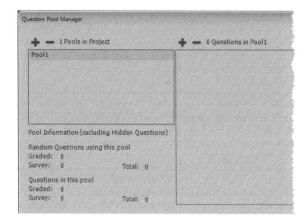

DESIGN TIP

Create a separate pool for each learning objective. That way, you know each objective will be represented in the project.

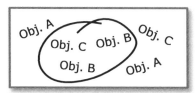

Three questions pulled from one group

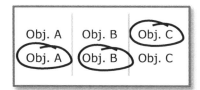

One question pulled from three groups

Add Questions to a Question Pool

To add a question to a pool:

1. Click the **Quiz** menu.

2. Select **Question Pool Manager**.

3. On the left, select the pool you want to add questions to.

4. Click the **Plus** button above the pane on the right.

5. Select the type and number of questions you want to add.

6. Click **Close** in the **Insert Question** dialog box.

7. Click **Close** in the **Question Pool Manager**.

You can add and delete pools and questions from the pool at any time by using the **Plus** and **Minus** buttons:

- Add and delete pools **(A)**

- Add and delete questions **(B)**

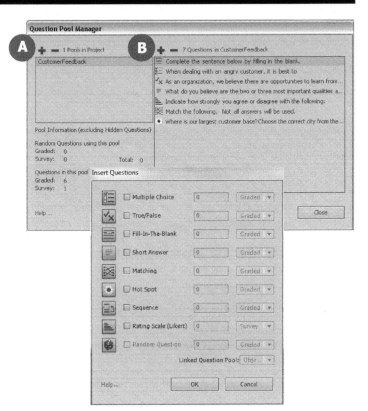

Managing Questions in the Question Pool

Remember that questions in a question pool are not added to your project, and therefore cannot be found in your **Filmstrip**. Instead, you can work with the questions from the **Question Pool** pane, found at the bottom of the interface. If the **Question Pool** pane isn't visible, you can go to the **Window** menu to add it.

From the **Question Pool** pane, you can:

- Select a question to show it in the work area so you can work on the question.

- Click the **Add Question** link to add a new question to that pool.

- Click the drop-down menu to move between the different pools associated with this project.

- Click the **Browse** button to bring up the **Question Pool Manager** dialog box.

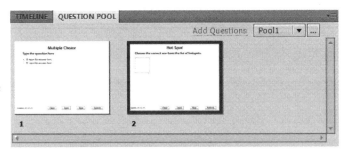

 TIME SAVER

You can import question pools from other projects. Just go to the **Quiz** menu, select **Import Question Pools**, and find the pool you want to import.

Add a Question From a Pool to Your Project

To randomly pull questions from your pool into your project:

1. Click the **Quiz** or **Insert** menu.
2. Select **Question Slide**.
3. Select **Random Question**.
4. Enter the number of questions from the pool you want to pull.
5. From the drop-down menu, select the question pool you want to pull from.
6. Click **OK**.

When you add questions to your project from a question pool, they appear as placeholder slides. You are not able to edit the questions from the placeholders, because they do not represent a single question. If you want to edit the question, go to the **Question Pool** pane.

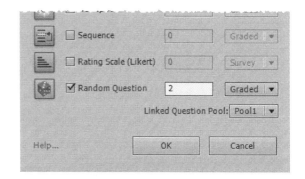

Use Quiz Templates

Quiz templates are free design templates you can use to make your quizzes more visually interesting. Each template is a Captivate project with one of each question type in it. Simply copy and paste the question slide from the template project to your project.

To use a quiz template:

1. Find the Adobe Captivate 5.5 software files on your computer (location varies based on your operating system).

2. Go to **Gallery** > **Quiz** > **Templates**.

3. Open the Captivate template file you want.

4. Copy the slide for the question type you want.

5. Paste it into your project.

6. In the template file, copy the master slide for the questions.

7. Paste the master slide into the **Master Slide** panel in your project.

8. Apply the question master to the question.

9. Configure the question as you normally would.

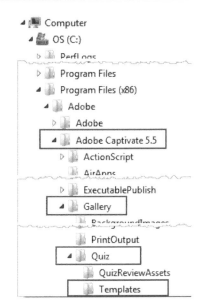

Slide Masters, p. 38

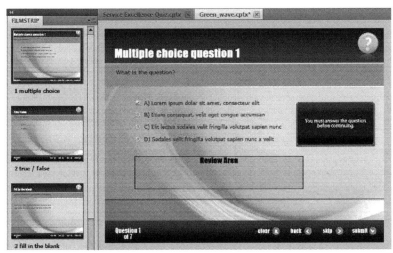

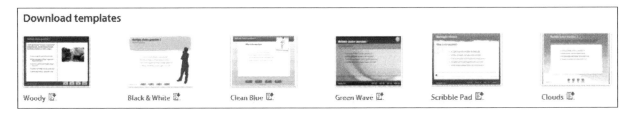

Download templates

Woody | Black & White | Clean Blue | Green Wave | Scribble Pad | Clouds

Quiz Results Slide

When you add the first quiz question to a project, Captivate adds a quiz results slide, showing the users how they did. You can make a number of changes to the results slide:

- Delete the slide if you don't want it. For example, if you just want a simple reinforcement question, you may not want a results slide.

- Move it to a different location in the project.

- Go to the **Quiz Properties** to turn various data elements on or off.

- Change the layout of the slide as you would any other slide. You can move elements, add elements, and delete elements. Be careful about making any changes to the text in brackets, as those are placeholders for the system-generated results.

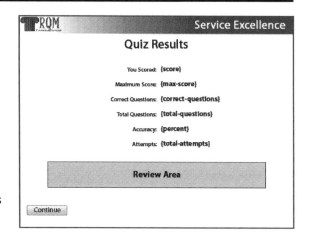

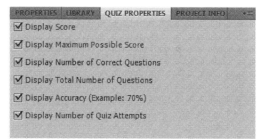

Change Quiz Preferences

To change the quiz preferences:

1. Go to the **Quiz** menu.

2. Select **Quiz Preferences**.

3. In the **Quiz** section, click each category, and change the settings you want.

4. Click the **OK** button.

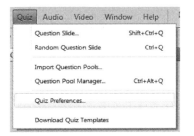

Reporting Category

The **Reporting** category governs how the quiz, and the course as a whole, interacts with a learning management system (LMS) or other tracking systems. This group of settings is covered in the Publishing chapter.

 Publishing, ch. 12

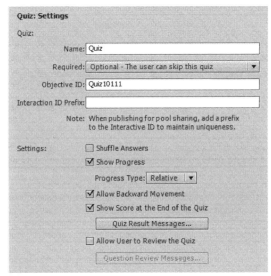

Settings Category

Name: Enter a name for the quiz, if needed.

Required: Indicate whether you want the student to be required to take the quiz. Options are:

- **Optional - The user can skip the quiz**
- **Required - The user must take the quiz to continue** (This means they have to click through all the slides in the quiz—it does not mean they have to pass or even answer the questions.)
- **Pass Required - The user must pass the quiz to continue**
- **Answer All - The user must answer every question to continue** (They do not have to pass, though.)

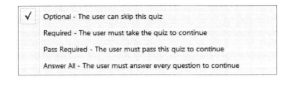

Objective ID: Use this field to identify the quiz to which a question slide belongs.

Interaction ID Prefix: To help you manage all the data tracked for quiz questions (answer on first attempt, answer on second attempt, etc.) you can assign a prefix that will go at the beginning of all the interaction IDs that are created for this quiz.

 Interaction ID, p. 159

Change Quiz Preferences (continued)

Settings Category (continued)

Shuffle Answers: This is a global setting for the entire quiz that shuffles the answers for any question type with multiple answers, such as multiple-choice questions. This can be overridden at the question level.

Show Progress: Check this box if you want to include a page count at the bottom of the question slides. Select **Relative** from the drop-down menu if you want to show the page number and the total number of pages in the quiz. Select **Absolute** if you only want to show the page number.

Allow Backward Movement: Uncheck this box if you want to remove the **Back** button from all the slides in the quiz. You can override this at the question level.

Show Score at the End of the Quiz: Uncheck this box if you do not want to include the **Quiz Results** slide. Check it again to bring it back.

Quiz Results Messages: Click this button to customize the appearance of the Quiz Results slide.

> **Messages**: Check the boxes if you want pass and fail messages to appear and customize the text, if needed.

> **Score**: Check or uncheck the boxes of the slide features you want. These options can also be changed by selecting the Quiz Results slide and clicking the **Quiz Properties** tab.

 Quiz Results Slide, p. 171

Allow User to Review the Quiz: Check this box if you want to add a **Review Quiz** button to the quiz results slide that lets students go back and review the questions, their answers, and the correct answers.

Question Review Messages: Click this button to customize the text shown to the student during the review. In Captivate 5.5, visual indicators are used to show the students the correct and incorrect answers. To make the course accessible to those using screen readers, you can enter the corresponding text used for the visual symbols.

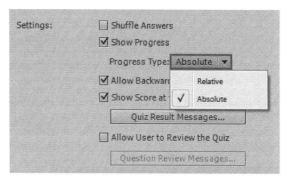

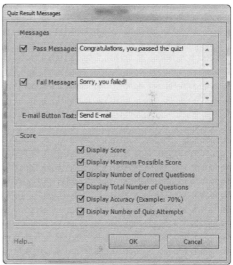

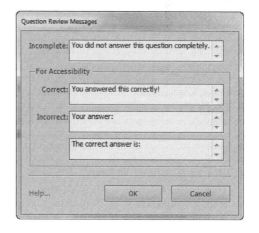

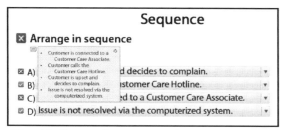

Visual indicators for correct and incorrect answers

Change Quiz Properties (continued)

Pass or Fail Category

Pass/Fail Options: Select the first radio button if you want to grade based on percentage or the second radio button to base it on raw score. Then enter the passing score for the score type you chose.

If Passing Grade: Select the action that you want to execute if the student achieves the passing score listed above. For example, you may want to branch to a certain slide.

If Failing Grade: Indicate what you want to have happen if the student does not achieve the passing score.

> **Number of Attempts**: Enter the number of attempts you want to give the student, or check the box if you want to provide infinite attempts.

> **Show Retake Button**: If you allow more than one attempt, check the box if you want to add a **Retake Quiz** button.

> **Action menu**: Select the action you want to execute if the student does not achieve the passing score.

If the student has not passed the test in the designated number of attempts, the **Retake Quiz** button disappears and the failing grade action is executed.

 Actions, ch. 7

Default Labels Category

This category lets you change all the default styles and messages for the buttons and feedback. For example, if you want to change what the success captions say when they first appear, you can modify the default here so that you don't have to change the tex on each and every slide.

 Styles, p. 98

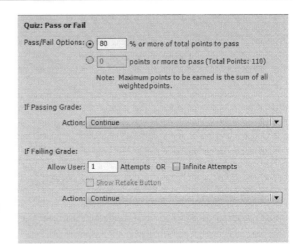

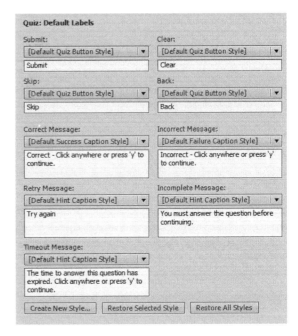

Special Tools & Wizards

11

Adobe Captivate comes with a number of special features designed to save you time and provide more options. In this chapter, you will learn about:

- **Aggregator Projects**: This lets you combine multiple projects into a single course.

- **Templates**: Templates help you save time and achieve a consistent look.

- **Mobile Project**: If you have the Adobe eLearning Suite, you can join the forces of Adobe Captivate and Adobe Device Central to create mobile projects.

- **Multi-SCORM Project**: With this option, you can combine Captivate projects and a few other output types in a combined course that works with learning management systems.

- **Spell Check**: Use this handy tool to check the spelling in captions, slide notes, slide names, text animations, and quizzes.

- **Find and Replace**: Search for certain words, any type of object, or any style of any object.

- **The Library**: The **Library** provides one convenient place to manage all the assets in your project.

- **Widgets**: Widgets are configurable SWF files that let you extend the capabilities of Captivate.

- **Sharing and Reviewing**: You can share files on Acrobat.com and use Adobe Captivate Reviewer to capture and manage feedback from reviewers.

- **Preferences**: You've learned about many preferences so far in the book. In this chapter, you'll learn about the ones that aren't covered in another chapter.

- **Exporting and Importing to XML**: XML files can let you do things outside of Captivate. For example, you can export to XML, translate some of the content or do a find/replace to update text, and then import the updated XML back into Captivate.

Notes

Aggregator Projects

An aggregator project lets you string together several different Captivate movies. For example, if you are creating a course on how to use a document management system, you might have five screen demonstrations, five practices, and a brief lesson on business rules. Rather than distributing these as individual courses, you can publish them all together as a single, complete course. Aggregator projects can be made up of multiple published SWFs created in Captivate.

 CAUTION

Aggregator projects can only contain published SWF files created in Captivate, not SWF files created elsewhere, such as in Flash. All files must be using the same version of ActionScript. You can see the version of ActionScript in the **Publish** dialog box for that project.

Create an Aggregator Project

To create an aggregator project:

1. Publish all the projects you want to include in the aggregator project.
2. Go to the **File** menu.
3. Select **New Project**.
4. Select **Aggregator Project**.
5. Click the **Add Module** (plus sign) button.
6. Find and select the published SWF you want to add.
7. Click the **Open** button.
8. Repeat steps 4-6 to add additional files.
9. Configure the settings.
10. Click the **Save** button to save the project.

Aggregator Project Settings

Master Movie: One of the movies can be designated as the master. The table of contents settings and project information for that movie will be used for the entire aggregator project. Select the movie you want to use as the default, and then check this box.

If you want to create movie information specific to this aggregator project and not pull it from any of the existing movies, click the **Info** button and add the movie information you want to use.

Movie Titles: Double-click the movie title in the list to rename it. If you don't want the movie title to appear in the published table of contents, select the movie and uncheck the **Include Module Title** check box.

Moving and Deleting Movies: To change the order of the movies, select a movie and click the up or down arrow buttons. To delete a movie, select it, and then click the **Delete** button.

Preview: Click this button to preview what the published project will look like.

Preloader: Click the **Browse** button to select a image to show when the published project is loading.

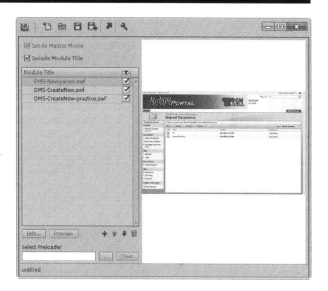

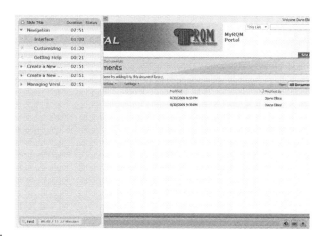

Published aggregator project with movie titles renamed and first movie expanded in the table of contents

Publish an Aggregator Project

To publish an aggregator project:

1. Click the **Publish Aggregator Project** button.
2. Select the output format you want.
3. Enter a name for the published project.
4. Enter or browse for the location where you want to save the published project.
5. Select the publishing settings you want.
6. Click the **Publish** button.

Publish Settings

Format: Select from Flash output (SWF), Windows-compatible executable file (EXE) or Mac-compatible executable file (APP).

Publish to Folder: Check this box if you want Captivate to create a separate folder for your published files.

Export to HTML: This option, checked by default, creates an HTML page and a JavaScript file that embed the SWF file into the HTML page. Uncheck it if you only want to publish the SWF file. Having the HTML page may be necessary based on how you plan to display the course.

Export PDF: Check this option to create a PDF document that plays the SWF file. Both PDF and SWF files are generated and both are needed to view the PDF.

Zip Files: Check this box if you want your published files to be zipped up into a .zip compressed folder.

Fullscreen: This option includes HTML files that cause the browser window to open up to its maximum size and hide browser elements such as the toolbar and **Favorites** bar.

Custom Icon: If you choose the **Win Executable** format, you can find and select an icon to associate with the executable file. This icon appears in the user's task bar and next to the file name in Windows Explorer.

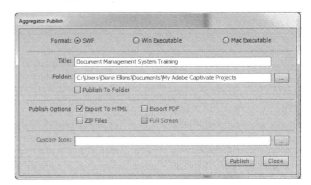

 CAUTION

Aggregator projects do not work with learning management systems. If you need to integrate with an LMS, use the Multi-SCORM Packager.

Multi-SCORM Packager, p. 182

Aggregator Preferences

There are additional aggregator settings in the **Aggregator Preferences** dialog box, which you can access by clicking the **Publish Settings** button.

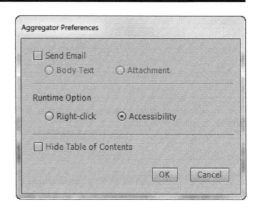

Send Email: Check this box if you want to have the project generate an email when the student finishes viewing it. You can either have the report data sent in the body of the email or as an attachment.

Runtime Options: If you'd like to enable right-click shortcuts for the student in the aggregator menu, select **Right-click**. However, the special logic needed to enable that right-click menu will disable accessibility features. So if you want the menu to be accessible, select that option instead.

 Accessibility, p. 216

Hide Table of Contents: Check this box if you want to turn off the table of contents completely in the published movie.

Manage Aggregator Files

You can open existing aggregator files from the main Captivate interface, or from the aggregator window if it is already open. Aggregator projects have a file extension of .aggr.

To open an aggregator file from Captivate:

1. Go to the **File** menu.
2. Select **New Project**.
3. Select **Aggregator Project**.
4. Click the **Open Aggregator Project** button.
5. Find and select the project you want.
6. Click the **Open** button.

If the aggregator window is already open, simply start with step 4.

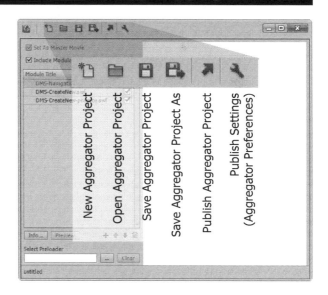

Templates

Templates help you create a consistent, professional look for your projects and help you save time in the development process. A Captivate template includes slides, objects, placeholder objects, placeholders for recording slides or question slides, master slides, styles, preferences, and slide notes. Project templates have a **.cptl** extension.

BRIGHT IDEA

Use slide notes to provide instructions on how to use the template.

For example, if you are creating a series of computer simulations, you can create a template that is set to the right size, has the toolbar configured the way you want it, is set up with all the default styles you'll want, and has introductory text and closing text placeholders. If you like to create branching scenarios, you can create a template that has all the pages set up with buttons branching to the different pages. Then all you have to do is add the content to the pages.

Create a Project Template

To create a project template:

1. Go to the **File** menu.
2. Select **New Project**.
3. Select **Project Template**. **(A)**
4. Select the size for the project. **(B)**
5. Click the **OK** button.
6. Add standard project elements.
7. Go to the **Insert** menu.
8. Select **Placeholder Objects** or **Placeholder Slides**.
9. Select the placeholders you want. **(C)**
10. Save the project.

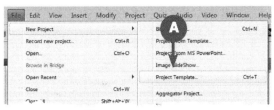

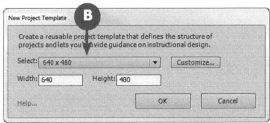

Standard Project Elements

You can add content and configure settings in a template much the same as any project. For example, add and delete slides, create slide masters, add objects to slides, such as text and images, set default styles, etc.

Placeholder Objects

In addition to standard elements, you can add placeholder objects. Placeholder objects put in a gray placeholder that you can fully format and configure properties for, but contains no actual content. When someone creates a project from the template, they can simply add the project-specific content to the placeholders quickly.

For example, if there is a caption at the end of each simulation that says "Click Next to continue," you could add it as a regular caption object with that text. However, if the closing message varies, you could put a caption placeholder with the settings you want, and then the developer of the project adds the project-specific text to the placeholder.

Placeholder Slides

A placeholder slide adds a slide to allow for either screen recording or quiz questions.

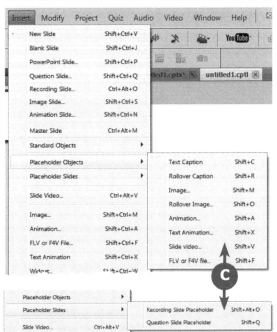

Create a New Project From a Template

To create a new project from a template:

1. Go to the **File** menu.
2. Select **New Project**.
3. Select **Project From Template**.

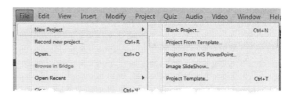

Modifying Standard Elements

When you create a project from a template, you can still add and modify content and settings like you would with any other project. For example, you can delete unwanted slides or add new ones, change the formatting or settings on objects, etc.

Modifying Placeholder Objects

To add your own content to placeholder objects, double-click the small icon in the bottom-right corner of the placeholder. The resulting steps vary based on the type of placeholder. For example, with a caption or rollover caption, the gray placeholder converts to an editable caption with the proper formatting, and with an image placeholder, the Open dialog box appears so you can find and select the image you want.

When you add content from placeholders, they appear with the settings indicated in the template. However, you can override those settings if you want to. For example, you could change the size of an image or the caption type of a caption.

Adding Questions and Screen Recordings

If you create a project from a template with slide placeholders, double-click the placeholder slide to either add questions or to initiate screen recording.

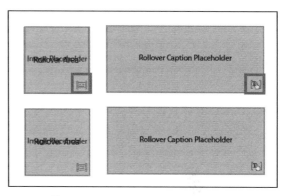

Rollover interaction template with image placeholders and rollover caption placeholders.

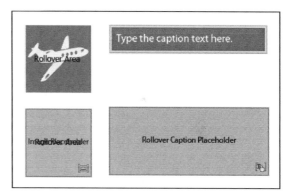

Interaction in a new project after adding one image and double-clicking the icon on the caption placeholder.

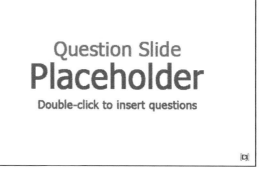

Create Mobile Projects

If you have the Adobe eLearning Suite, you can create an Adobe Captivate project for mobile devices. You can use Adobe Device Central (which is part of the eLearning Suite) to select the target mobile device when you create the project and then again to test the project once you've built it.

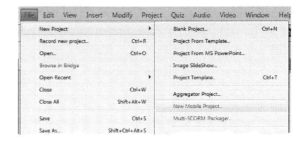

Create a Multi-SCORM Package

The Multi-SCORM Packager lets you combine multiple files into a single shareable courseware object (SCO) to be uploaded to an LMS. The SCO can contain one or more projects from Captivate as well as from Flash, Adobe Presenter, and quizzes made in Dreamweaver with the Coursebuilder extension.

 SCORM Publishing, p. 206

Check Spelling

The spell check feature in Captivate checks captions, slide notes, slide names, text animations, and quizzes.

 CAUTION

The spell checker does NOT check alt text added via the **Accessibility** button.

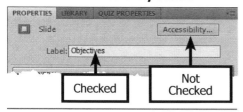

To check the spelling in your project:

1. Go to the **Project** menu.
2. Select **Check Spelling**.

Click the **Options** button to change the spell check settings, such as the default language and types of words to ignore.

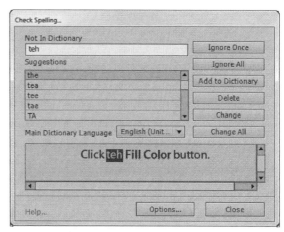

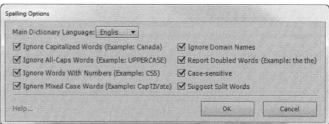

Find and Replace

Find and Replace lets you search for and replace text like you can in most word processing software. In addition, you can search for certain types of objects, such as rollover captions. This can make it easier to find something in a large project.

To find text or object types:

1. Go to the **Edit** menu.
2. Select **Find and Replace**.
3. In the **Search In** field, select the type of object you want to search in or for, or select **All Object Types**.
4. In the **Styles** field, select the styles you want to search in or for, if needed.
5. In the **Find** field, enter the text you want to look for, if needed.
6. In the **Replace** field, enter the text you want to replace the found text with, if needed.
7. Check and uncheck the boxes at the bottom to limit or expand your search.
8. Click one of the four buttons on the right to initiate the search or replacement.

Find, **Replace**, **Whole Word**, and **Match Case** are only available if your search includes text-related objects.

The Library

The **Library** contains all the assets of a project: those currently in use, those added but no longer in use, and those added but not yet used. The **Library** is unique to that project. For example, the **Library** contains:

- The background image and audio of all current slides.
- The background image and audio of all deleted slides.
- Every version of the background image and audio of a certain slide.
- An image or audio clip you added to the Library and then added to a slide.
- An image or audio you added to the Library that has not yet been used on a slide.

The default location for the **Library** is the panel on the right side of the interface. Look for a tab next to the **Properties** tab. If it is not showing, go to the **Window** menu, and select **Library**.

What can you do with the **Library**?

- Store assets that you know you'll need later.
- Revert back to previous versions of an asset.
- Reuse assets over and over.
- Edit assets.
- Import and export assets.
- Update linked assets, such as a linked PowerPoint or video file.

You can also view important information about your project assets from the Library. For example, you can:

Preview the assets: When you select an item in the **Library**, a preview appears in the pane at the top. For audio, video, and animations, click the **Play** button **(A)** to play the media.

Determine if assets are currently in use: The **Use Count** column **(B)** shows you how many times an item is being used the project. A **0** indicates an unused item.

Sort the assets: Click a column heading **(C)** to sort the assets by that heading.

Organize into folders: Right-click an item and select **New Folder** to create a new folder. Then drag and drop items into that folder. New folders go inside an existing media type and cannot contain different media types.

The Library contains:

Audio

Backgrounds

Images

Media

  Animations

  Video

Presentations

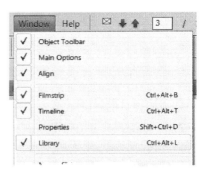

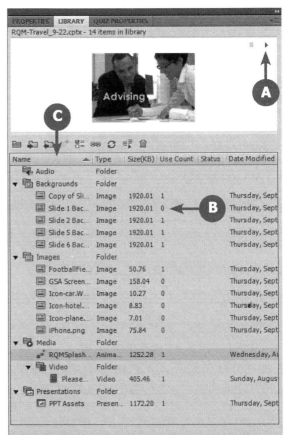

Manage Assets in the Library

You can perform these functions in the **Library** by right-clicking an asset or selecting it and using a button at the top.

To delete an asset:
- Right-click the asset, and select **Delete**. -or-
- Select the asset, and click the **Delete** button.

To delete all unused assets:
- Click the **Select Unused** button, and then click the **Delete** button.

To edit an asset:
- Right-click the asset, and select **Edit with**. -or-
- Select the asset, and click the **Edit** button.

To rename an asset:
- Right-click the asset, and select **Rename**.

To update a linked asset:
- Right-click the asset, and select **Update**. -or-
- Select the asset, and click the **Update** button.

 Update Project Video, p. 79
Update an Imported Slide, p. 33

To reuse an asset:
- Drag it to the slide you want.

To export an asset:
- Right-click the asset, and select **Export**. -or-
- Select the asset, and click the **Export** button.

To import an asset into the Library:
- Right-click any asset, and select **Import**. -or-
- Click the **Import** button.

To import an asset from another Library:
1. Click the **Open Library** button.
2. Find and select the Captivate project with the library you want to use.
3. Click the **Open** button.
4. In the pop-up window, find and select the asset you want to import.
5. Drag the asset to a slide or a folder in the Library.

Once you import assets from another project, that project is available from a drop-down menu on the **Open Library** button.

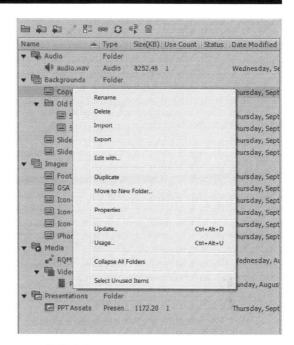

Open Library | Import | Export | Edit | Properties | Usage | Update | Select Unused | Delete

 # CAUTION

The **Library** contains all versions of all assets. That can cause problems if:

- You deleted an asset from a slide because there was a problem with it, and then accidentally reuse it.
- You had sensitive information that you covered with merged objects, but the original image with the sensitive information is still in the **Library**.
- You are concerned about the file size of the .cptx file. (Library size does not affect the published movie, just the source file.)

For all these reasons, it is a good idea to regularly delete unneeded assets.

Widgets

Widgets are configurable Flash objects that can be configured in Captivate without using Flash. Widgets let you enhance and expand the capabilities of Captivate. You can get widgets in one of three ways:

- Use widgets installed with Captivate.
- Download additional widgets from Adobe or third-party sources.
- Create your own in Adobe Flash.

Widgets are configured in two places. With most widgets, a **Widget Properties** dialog box appears when you add the widget. This lets you choose many of the key settings for that widget. In addition, you can configure many of the regular properties in the **Properties** panel. For example, with a button widget, you designate the style and text in the **Widget Properties** dialog box, but you still designate the button actions in the regular **Properties** panel.

Add a Widget From the Properties Panel

Certain object types have a link to widgets right in the **Properties** panel. This link lets you select from any of the widgets installed in the Captivate program files. For example, if you add a button, the button's **Properties** panel lets you use a button widget.

To add a widget from the Properties panel:

1. Add the object type you want.
2. Click the widget link in the **Properties** panel. **(A)**
3. In the **Widgets** panel that appears, click the **Insert** link for the widget you want to add. **(B)**
4. Configure the properties in the **Widget Properties** dialog box. **(C)**
5. Click **OK**.

BRIGHT IDEAS

- Pre-installed widgets can be found in the Captivate program files on your hard drive.

  Adobe > Captivate 5.5 > Gallery > Widgets

- You can bring up the **Widgets** panel any time you want by going to the **Window** menu and selecting **Widgets**.

- After you've added the widget, you can still go back and edit the properties found in the **Widget Properties** dialog box. Click the **Widget Properties** button in the object's **Properties** panel.

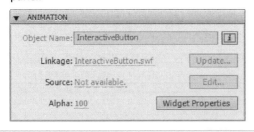

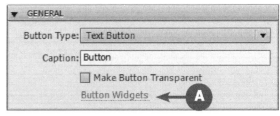

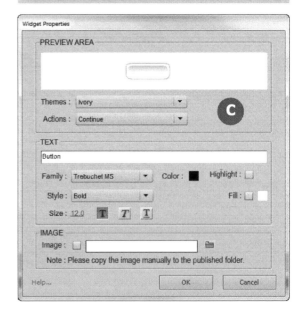

Add a Widget From the Insert Menu

When you add a widget from the **Insert** menu, you can select any widget on your computer or a network drive. This can include the pre-installed widgets that come with Captivate, third-party widgets you've downloaded, or custom-created widgets.

To add a widget from the Insert menu:

1. Go to the **Insert** menu.
2. Select **Widgets**.
3. Find and select the widget you want.
4. Click the **Open** button.
5. Configure the widget properties.
6. Click **OK**.

POWER TIPS

- Use the buttons at the bottom of the **Widgets** panel to help manage widgets.

Change Path: The **Widgets** panel pulls from the widgets stored in the Captivate program files. Click this button if you want to pull from a different file location.

Adobe Captivate Exchange: Click this button or the **More** link on the end to go to the Adobe Captivate Exchange website to find additional widgets to download.

Browse: Click this button to find and select additional widgets to add to the panel.

Refresh: Click this button to refresh the view of available widgets.

Filter: Use the drop-down menu to filter the view of available widgets.

- You can create your own widgets in Adobe Flash. Go to the **File** menu, select **New Project**, and then **Widget in Flash**. This option only works if you have Adobe Flash installed on your computer. Refer to the Adobe Captivate 5.5 help manual for more information.

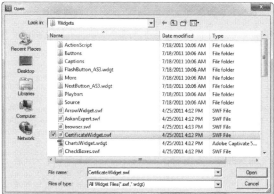

Sharing and Reviewing

Acrobat.com is an online collaboration site from Adobe that offers online meetings, document sharing, and file storage. You can either upload or share your Captivate files to Acrobat.com in published format (SWF) or in source file format (CPTX). If you do not already have an Acrobat.com account, you can register for one at www.acrobat.com.

You can also use Adobe Captivate Reviewer to capture comments from reviewers to help you manage the review and editing process more easily. This can either be done through Acrobat.com or your own network.

Upload Files to Acrobat.com

To upload files to Acrobat.com:

1. Go to the **File** menu.

2. Select **Collaborate**.

3. Select **Upload Files to Acrobat.com**.

4. Enter your Adobe ID and password.

5. Click the **Sign In** button.

6. Enter the name you want to use for the file.

7. Check the box(es) for the version(s) of the file you want to upload.

8. Click the **Upload** button.

The files are available from your Acrobat.com home page on the **Files** tab and can be viewed by anyone with access to that page.

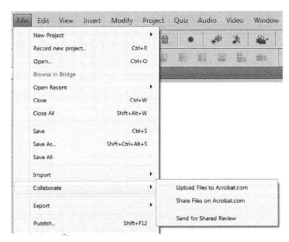

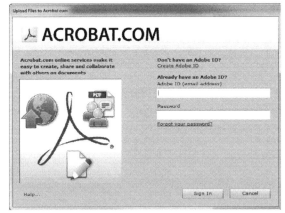

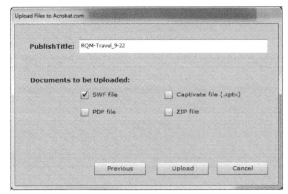

Share Files on Acrobat.com

The process of sharing files is very similar to the process for uploading files. This procedure also uploads the file to your Acrobat.com account, but in addition, it sends an email to anyone you want to share the file with.

To share files from Acrobat.com:

1. Go to the **File** menu.
2. Select **Collaborate**.
3. Select **Share Files on Acrobat.com**.
4. Enter your Adobe ID and password.
5. Click the **Sign In** button.
6. Enter the name you want to use for the file.
7. Check the box(es) for the version(s) of the files you want to upload.
8. Click the **Next** button.
9. Enter the address, subject line, and message for the email to be sent to the person you are sharing the file with.
10. Click the **SEND** button.

The uploaded file appears on your Acrobat.com home page on the **Files** tab, and the person you are sharing with receives an email with a link to view the file. In order to view it, the person must sign in with their own Adobe ID.

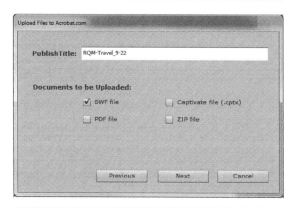

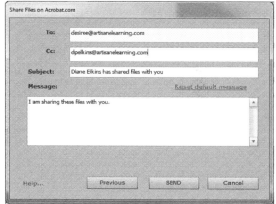

Adobe Captivate Reviewer

When you send a file for shared review, you are able to collect feedback on the project. Reviewers can view the project in a special interface that lets them add comments. Your reviewers must first install Adobe AIR and then install Adobe Captivate Reviewer to view the project and add comments. You can then accept, reject, or ask for feedback on the comments.

To send for shared review:

1. Go to the **File** menu.
2. Select **Collaborate**.
3. Select **Send for Shared Review**.
4. Enter a name for the file.
5. Select the comment collection method you want.
6. Click the **Next** button.
7. Enter your Adobe ID and password.
8. Click the **Sign In** button.
9. Enter the address, subject line, and message for the email to be sent to the person you are sharing the file with.
10. Click the **SEND** button.

Collection Methods

Acrobat.com: With this method, a Captivate review file (.crev) is stored on Acrobat.com, and an email is sent to reviewers with a link to the review file.

Internal Server: With this method, you either place the files in a shared location, such as a network drive, or you can email the review file and have the reviewers export their comments and email them back to you. (You can then import them into your review file.)

There are a few extra steps after step 8. You will pick where to save the review file and comments file and whether or not you want the system to send an email. That email can include the review file as an attachment as well as a link to Adobe Captivate Reviewer.

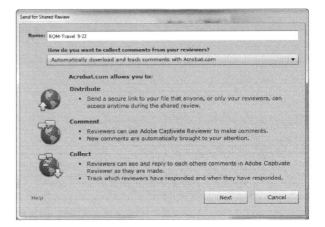

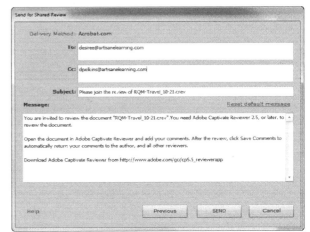

 BRIGHT IDEA

Refer to the Adobe Captivate 5.5 help documentation for more information on how to use the Captivate Reviewer. (Search for "Reviewing Adobe Captivate projects.")

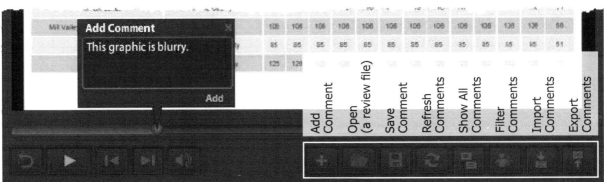

Adobe Captivate Reviewer (continued)

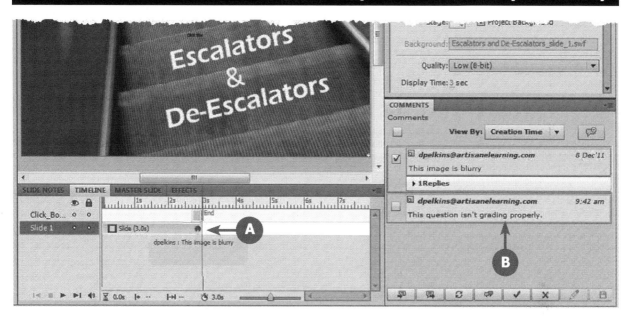

Comments can be managed in the Adobe AIR application or directly in your Captivate project. To view them in Captivate, first go to the **Window** menu, and select **Comments**.

- In the **Timeline**, a dot appears for each comment. Hover over the dot to read the comment. **(A)**

- In the **Comments** pane, you can view all the comments for the project, using the **View By** menu to sort by time, reviewer, or status. **(B)**

- In the **Filmstrip**, a comments icon appears to let you know there is a comment for that slide. **(C)**

The **Comments** pane also has a number of buttons at the bottom to help you manage the comments. For some commands, you need to first check the box next to the comment you want to manage.

Import Comments: Use this to incorporate comments that others exported for you.

Export Comments: Use this to create a backup file or to share with another user.

Refresh Comments: If reviewers are using one of the online methods for adding their comments, click this button to incorporate the most recent comments.

Reply: Click this button to type a response to a comment.

Accept: Click this button to change the status to "Accepted." You can include a message here.

Reject: Click this button to change the status to "Rejected." You can include a message here.

Edit Comments: Click this button to edit a comment.

Save Comments: Click this button to save comments.

Import Comments	Export Comments	Refresh Comments	Reply	Accept	Reject	Edit Comments	Save Comments

CAUTION

The **End Review** button is not for ending a particular review session. It is for ending the entire review cycle by deleting all of the comments. Only click this button if you are sure you want to delete all of the comments.

Preferences

The **Preferences** window has important settings ranging from quality and project defaults to publishing and reporting. You can get to the preferences from the **Edit** menu. In addition, many menus have shortcuts that take you directly to a certain tab. For example, **Quiz Preferences** on the **Quiz** menu opens up the **Preferences** window with the **Quiz Reporting** tab showing.

In this book, most of the preferences are covered in the chapter relating to that type of preferences. The remainder are covered here.

- Recording preferences: chapter 2
- Project preferences: chapter 12
- Quiz preferences: chapter 10

General Settings

Show Welcome Screen: When you have Captivate open but no projects open, you see the **Welcome** screen. If you don't want to see it, uncheck this box.

Rescale Imported/Pasted Slides: If you import or paste a slide into a project, and the item being added is larger than the project, Captivate asks if you want to resize it. Check this box if you want Captivate to resize it without asking.

Generate Project Backup: Check this box if you want Captivate to create a backup file of your project. It is saved with a .bak extension. Change the extension back to .cptx to restore the file.

Default Locations

> **Publish At**: This is where published projects will be saved, unless you change the location. Click the **Browse** button and select a new location if you want projects to publish to a different location by default.

> **Project Cache**: Software uses cache to temporarily store data to help speed up processing. This field indicates what location is being used for cache.

> **Clear Cache**: If you are having performance problems, you can clear your cache by clicking here.

> **Comments At**: If you use Adobe Captivate Reviewer, this is where the comments will be saved. Click the **Browse** button to save them to a different location.

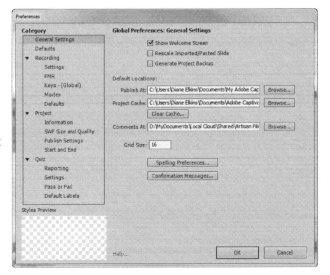

Grid Size: You can use an on-screen grid to help line up objects on slide. Change the number to make grid lines closer (smaller #) or farther apart (larger #).

Spelling Preferences: Click this button to change spell check preferences, such as what language to use and what types of words to check vs. ignore.

Confirmation Messages: Captivate displays various confirmation messages, such as when you delete a slide or an object. Click this button to turn certain types of messages on or off.

Welcome screen

Confirmation messages

Default Settings

Slide Duration: This is how long all slides are when they are first added to the project. Change the length (in seconds) if you prefer a different default length.

Background Color: By default, all new slides have a white background. Change the color here if you want a different default background color.

Preview Next: When you preview a project, one of the options is to preview a small chunk of slides—five by default. If you would like that menu option to preview a different number of slides, enter that number here.

Object Defaults: In this section, you can designate the length (in seconds) for how long certain objects should appear when they are first added to a project. For example, all text captions are three seconds long when they are first added to the project. If you would like to change the default length, select an object from the first drop-menu and set up the length just beneath that. You can also designate a default style for the selected object. Click the **Restore Selected** or **Restore All** buttons to go back to the previously saved settings.

 Styles, p. 105

Autosize Buttons: When you create a text button, the button resizes automatically based on how long the text is. Uncheck this box if you do not want the buttons to resize.

Autosize Captions: When you change the text in a caption, the caption resizes automatically to accommodate the changes in the text. Uncheck this box if you do not want the captions to resize.

Calculate Caption Timing: By default, captions use the length specified in the **Object Defaults** section above when they are added to a project. Check this box if you want the length to be determined by Captivate based on how much text is in the caption. A caption with more text will stay up longer, giving the student more time to read it.

 # BRIGHT IDEA

If you have a project open when you change the defaults, the changes apply only to that project. If you change them when there are no projects open, they become global preferences for all new projects.

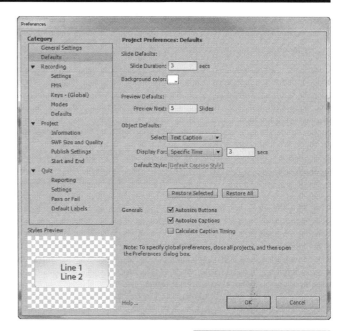

Exporting and Importing to XML

Exporting to XML, or extensible markup language, is a way to convert your Captivate project to a text-based form that can be translated, imported into other software applications, or re-imported back into Captivate.

```
<group datatype="plaintext" cp:datatype="x-property" restype="x-cp-slide-label" extype="337">
   <trans-unit id="911-337">
      <source>Standard Fill</source>
   </trans-unit>
</group>
<group datatype="plaintext" cp:datatype="x-property" restype="x-cp-slide-accessibility"
extype="1285">
   <trans-unit id="911-1285">
      <source> </source>
   </trans-unit>
</group>
<group cp:datatype="x-object" restype="x-cp-audio-item" id="1409" extype="275">
   <group cp:datatype="x-object" restype="x-cp-closed-caption-items" id="1410" extype="113">
      <group cp:datatype="x-object" restype="x-cp-closed-caption-item" id="1442"
      extype="114">
         <group datatype="plaintext" cp:datatype="x-property" restype="x-cp-closed-caption-
         name" extype="207">
            <trans-unit id="1442-207">
               <source>Adding a fill color to your cells can make your spreadsheets more
               visually interesting. But it can also make them easier to understand. By
               adding a fill color to header rows or cells with key information, you can
               make the important elements stand out. </source>
            </trans-unit>
         </group>
      </group>
   </group>
</group>
<group cp:datatype="x-object" restype="x-cp-items" id="912" extype="69">
   <group cp:datatype="x-object" restype="Text Caption" id="1462" extype="19">
      <group cp:datatype="x-paragraph" css-style="line-spacing:1.00;line-indent:0.00">
         <trans-unit id="1462-19-1">
            <source>
               <g id="1462-19-1-1" css-style="font-family:'Myriad Pro';font-
               face:'Regular';color:#333333;font-size:18.0pt" ctype="x-cp-font">Select
               the cells you want to format.</g>
            </source>
```

Export to XML

To export a project to XML:

1. Go to the **File** menu.
2. Select **Export**.
3. Select **To XML**.
4. Find and select the location where you want to save the file.
5. Click the **Save** button.

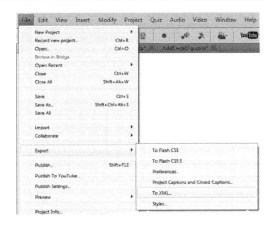

Import to XML

To import a project from XML:

1. Go to the **File** menu.
2. Select **Import**.
3. Select **From XML**.
4. Find and select the file you want to import.
5. Click the **Open** button.

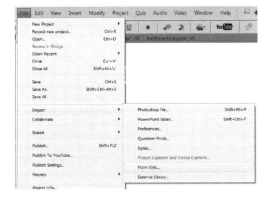

Publishing 12

In this chapter, you will learn about the various settings that affect your finished output, such as:

- Whether to include a control toolbar that lets the student control the progress of the finished movie.
- Whether to send tracking data to a learning management system (LMS).
- How much to compress the output to accommodate slow connection speeds.

In addition, you'll look at the specific publishing formats:

- Flash (SWF)
- Adobe Connect
- Media (EXE, APP, MP4)
- E-mail or FTP delivery of files (published files or source files)
- Print (Microsoft Word)

In this chapter:
- Rescale a Project
- Project Skins
- Project Settings
- Reporting Settings
- Publishing Options

Notes

Rescale a Project

When you publish your project, the output size is the same as the project size. If you need your published movie to be smaller, you need to resize the entire project.

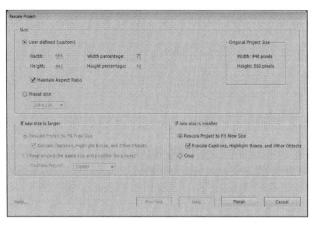

To rescale a project:

1. Go to the **Modify** menu.
2. Select **Rescale project**.
3. Set the new size by width/height dimensions, width height percentage, or preset sizes from a menu.
4. Set the options for larger or smaller projects.
5. Click **Finish**.

If new size is larger

Rescale Project: Select this option if you want to enlarge the entire background image to fit in the new size. Check the box underneath if you want to resize all objects accordingly. Otherwise, they will stay the same size.

Keep project the same size: Select this option if you want to keep the background image and objects at 100%, meaning it will be smaller than the project window. If you select this option, use the **Position Project** drop-down menu to indicate where in the larger window you want the project to appear (center, top left, etc.)

If new size is smaller

Rescale Project: Select this option if you want to scale down the entire background image to fit in the new size. Check the box underneath if you want to resize all objects accordingly. Otherwise, they will stay the same size.

Crop: Select this option if you want to keep the background image and objects at 100% of their current size, but instead crop off whatever doesn't fit in the new size. If you select this option, the **Next** button becomes active, letting you indicate what part to keep and what part to crop.

 CAUTION

- If you select the crop option, make sure you are not cropping out key areas of the slide.
- Be careful about resizing a project to be larger. You will lose resolution, and the resulting quality may not be what you want.

 BRIGHT IDEAS

- Make sure you really need to resize a project, as you might be able to resize it in its final destination. For example, if you will place the finished project in another e-learning authoring tool, you may be able to resize the published movie right on the page.
- Cropping a project is helpful if you want to remove part of what you captured, such as the menus and toolbars at the top of a web-based application.
- It is a good idea to keep a copy of your Captivate file at full size. Once you resize the project, it may be difficult to go back and get additional captures if you need changes.

Configure Project Skin

The project skin controls three features: the playback controls, a border, and a table of contents.

To select an existing skin:

1. Click the **Project** menu.
2. Select **Skin Editor**.
3. Select the option you want from the **Skin** drop-down menu.
4. Close the window.

To change the project skin:

5. Click the **Project** menu.
6. Select **Skin Editor**.
7. Configure the playback control settings you want.
8. Click the **Border** button.
9. Configure the border settings you want.
10. Click the **Table of Contents** button.
11. Configure the table of contents settings you want.
12. Close the window.

Playback Control Options

Show Playback Control: Check this box if you want to provide the student with a toolbar that controls the movie.

Playbar Overlay: By default, the playbar appears under the published movie. If you check this box, the playbar is placed over the movie. This does cover up part of the content area, but it keeps the published size exactly the same as the project size.

Playbar: From the drop-down menu, select the playbar style you want.

 **Web Resource:**
Printable playbar guide

Playbar Widgets: Click this link to open the **Widgets** pane in the **Properties** dialog box to find other playbar styles.

Position: Indicate where in the movie you want the playbar to appear: top, left, bottom, or right.

Layout: Indicate the size and more specific position of the playbar, such as stretched across the screen or over to the left or right. Options vary based on what you choose in the **Position** menu.

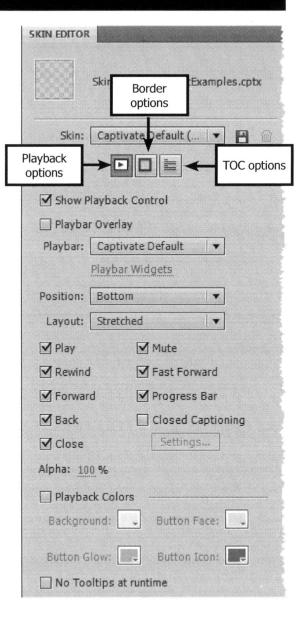

 TIME SAVER

If you customize your skin settings, you can save them to reuse over and over. Click the **Save** button next to the name of the skin to add it to the drop-down list for later use.

Configure Project Skin (continued)

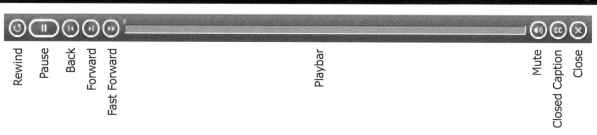

Rewind | Pause | Back | Forward | Fast Forward | Playbar | Mute | Closed Caption | Close

Button Options: Check the box for each option you want to include on your playbar.

Alpha: Indicate how opaque or transparent you want the playbar to be. 100% is fully opaque. Lower numbers are semi-transparent.

Playback Colors: To further customize the playbar, check this box and then use the color swatches to adjust the color of the different elements.

No Tooltips at Runtime: By default, when a student rolls his or her mouse over a toolbar button, a small tooltip appears explaining what the button is for. Check this box if you don't want the tooltips.

Border Options

Click the **Borders** button **(A)** to configure a border around the published movie. The skin you have selected in the **Skin** drop-down menu affects what the default options are.

Show Borders: Check this box if you want to have a border around your project. Then, click the button for each side that you want to have a border for. (Click all four for a full border.)

Style: Indicate if you want the border to have square or round corners.

Texture: For a patterned border, select from one of almost 100 texture/pattern options, such as brushed metal or wood grain.

Width: Enter the point size for the border width.

Color: Click the swatch to change the color of the border. (The color chosen here does not affect any textures used.)

HTML Background: Click the swatch to change the color of the background area around the project.

 POWER TIP

You can make your own custom playbar in Flash. See the Captivate User's Manual for specifications.

 CAUTION

Tooltips are also read by screen readers. If you turn off the tooltips, then your course will not be Section 508 compliant.

Be sure to enable the **Closed Caption** option for accessible projects.

 Accessibility, p. 216

Skin: CoolBlue (Modified) ▼

☑ Show Borders

Style: Square Edge ▼
Texture: None ▼
Width: 13
Color: ▮
HTML Background: ▯

Configure Project Skin (continued)

Table of Contents Options

Click the **Table of Contents** button **(A)** to configure the table of contents. The skin you have selected in the **Skin** drop-down menu affects what the default options are.

Show TOC: Check this box if you want your published file to have a table of contents that lets the student move freely around the course.

Title: Double-click a slide title to edit the name.

Show/Hide TOC Entries: Check or uncheck the box in the show/hide column (with the eyeball icon) to show or hide that slide in the table of contents.

Buttons

These options change how your slides appear in the table of contents. They do not affect how the slides appear in the project itself (such as deleting them or rearranging them).

Folder: Click the **Folder** button to create a topic name entry in the table of contents.

Reset TOC: Click this button to return the settings to their original configuration.

Move TOC Entry Left/Right: Use the left and right arrows to indent or outdent the selected slide.

Move TOC Entry Up/Down: Use the up and down arrows to change the order of the entries. You can also click and drag the slides to rearrange them.

Delete TOC Entry: To delete a topic name, select that line item and then click the **Delete** button. You cannot delete a slide using the **Delete** button.

 CAUTION

Changes made to your project after you create the Table of Contents are not automatically updated in the TOC. Instead, come back to this dialog box and click the **Reset** button.

Project Info

Click the **Info** button to add project information such as project name, author, and description. This information appears in a pop-up window at the top of the TOC.

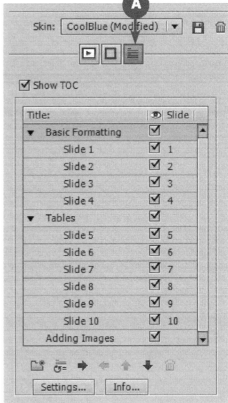

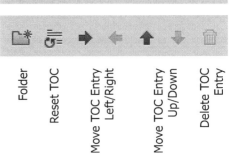

Configure Project Skin (continued)

TOC Settings

Click the **Settings** button to bring up the **TOC Settings** dialog box.

Style: Select **Overlay** to have the TOC appear on the slide with a small show/hide icon that lets the student show or hide it. Select **Separate** if you want the TOC to appear to the side of the slide.

Position: Indicate if you want the TOC to be on the left or right side of the slide.

Color: Click the swatches to change the color for the various elements of the TOC panel.

Alpha: By default, the TOC is fully opaque. Enter a lower number for semi-transparency.

Runtime Options

Collapse All: When checked, all folders in the TOC will be collapsed when the project plays.

Self-Paced Learning: When checked, the student's flags are not reset when the project is closed, and, upon return, the student may resume where he or she left off previously.

Show Duration: Check this box if you want the slide duration to appear next to each slide. Uncheck it if you don't.

Enable Navigation: When checked, the student can move around freely using the TOC. Uncheck this if you do not want the student to be able to navigate via the TOC.

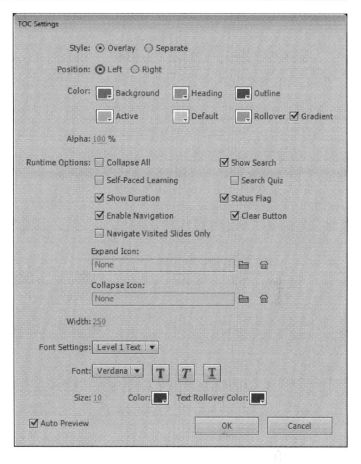

Navigate Visited Slides Only: When checked, students can navigate freely around any slide they have already visited, but can't jump ahead in the course. This option is only available if you have **Enable Navigation** checked.

Show Search: Check this box if you want a search box in the TOC. Check the **Search Quiz** box if you want to include quiz slides in the search.

Status Flag: When this option is selected, a check mark appears next to each slide that the user has completed viewing.

Clear Button: If checked, the student can clear his or her status.

Expand/Collapse Icon: When there are folders, the TOC uses traditional triangle icons for expanding and collapsing the sections. If you want to import your own image, you can do that here.

Width: Enter the width you want for the TOC, in pixels.

Font Options: The TOC keeps font formatting settings for up to four levels. To change the fonts, first select the level you want to change in the **Font Settings** drop-down menu. Then, select the font style, size, color, and effects (bold, italic, underline, and rollover).

Auto Preview: Uncheck this option if you do not want to see the changes in the preview panel while you are making them.

Change Project Preferences

The **Preferences** dialog box has a number of settings that affect your output. You can:

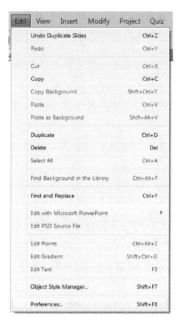

- Add information about the project, such as the title, author, and description.

- Adjust size and quality settings.

- Indicate which features you want to include, such as audio and mouse click sounds.

- Indicate how you want the published movie to start and end.

- Configure options for reporting scores and completion status to a learning management system or other reporting system.

To change the project preferences:

1. Go to the **Edit** menu.
2. Select **Preferences**.
3. Click the category you want to change.
4. Make your changes.
5. Click **OK**.

Project Information Settings

Project information provides data about the project, such as the title, author, etc. This can be used as internal information for the developers, included in a table of contents for the student to see, or read by screen readers in an accessible project.

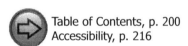

Table of Contents, p. 200
Accessibility, p. 216

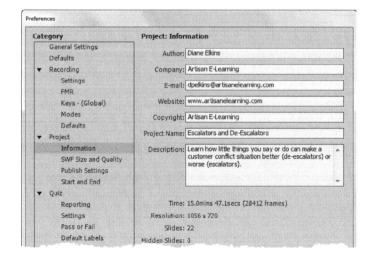

SWF Size and Quality Settings

When publishing your project, you'll want to balance quality with file size. A high-quality output may look good, but may be too large for remote viewers to access easily. Conversely, a small output file may be easy to access but may not look or sound good.

Compress Full Motion Recording SWF file: If you have any full-motion recording in your project, then your movie contains video. Check this box if you want to compress that video.

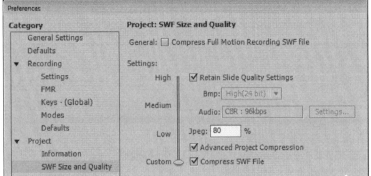

High, Medium, and Low: Set the slider at any of these positions for settings which provide that level of quality for audio and video.

Custom: Set the slider at this level if you want to set each quality setting individually.

Retain Slide Quality Settings: Check this box if you want to manage quality at the slide level. Or, uncheck it and enter settings for the entire project here.

Bmp: Select high or low quality for the screenshots taken during your capture session.

Audio: Click the **Settings** button to change the audio quality of any voiceover, music, etc.

Jpeg: Select a compression percentage for any JPG images you placed on your slides.

Advanced Project Compression: If you check this option, Captivate looks for similarities between slides and publishes only the differences as the project goes from slide to slide. Be sure to check your output with this option to make sure everything renders properly.

Compress SWF File: If you select **High**, **Medium**, or **Low**, this box is checked, meaning additional compression is used (other than the options listed above). If you don't want that extra compression, uncheck the box.

Publish Settings

Frames Per Second: To create the movie effect, Captivate publishes at 30 frames per second. You may need to change this if you are embedding your SWF movie into another file that uses a different rate.

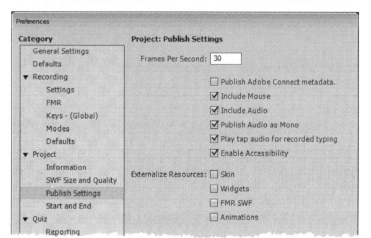

Publish Adobe Connect metadata: Selecting this option makes it easier to integrate your movie with Adobe Connect.

Include Mouse: Keep this checked if you want the slide mouse movements to appear in the published movie.

Include Audio: Keep this checked if you want to publish any audio that you've added to the project.

Publish Audio as Mono: This setting converts stereo audio to mono audio, resulting in a smaller file size. With voiceover narration, mono audio is a good way to reduce file size without sacrificing audio quality.

Play tap audio for recorded typing: If you captured any typing in your project, keep this box checked if you want the published file to play keyboard tapping sounds. Uncheck the box if you don't want to hear those sounds.

Enable Accessibility: Check this box to make your movie compatible with screen readers and to enable any other accessibility features you set up.

Externalize Resources: By default, your movie publishes as a single SWF file that includes the skin, widgets, full motion video, and added animations. If you prefer to have these objects published as separate files (referred to by the SWF file), then check the box for that object type. This can help with download times for extremely large files.

Start and End Settings

Auto Play: By default, a published movie starts playing immediately upon being downloaded. Uncheck the box if you don't want it to autostart. If it is not set to autostart, a play button appears on the first frame for the student to click. If you want to select your own play button, click the **Browse** button.

Preloader: The preloader is a small image or animation that plays while the movie is downloading. With larger movies or slower connections, preloaders are helpful as they let students know that the movie is downloading.

Preload %: This indicates the percentage of the movie that must be downloaded before it starts playing.

Password Protect Project: Use this option if you want students to enter a password before they can view the movie. Click the **Options** button to change the system messages regarding the password.

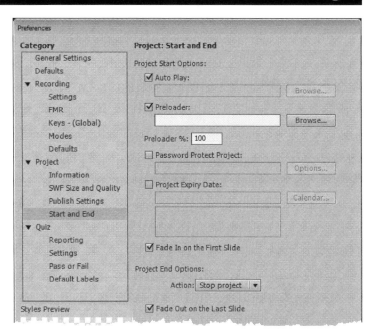

Project Expiry Date: Check this option and enter a date if you want your movie to expire after a certain date. An expired movie cannot be viewed. This can be useful for limited-time offers or policy/legal information that changes yearly.

Fade In on the First Slide: Select this option to have the first frame of your movie fade in.

Project End Options: Use this drop-down menu to designate what action should happen when the movie is finished, such as stopping, looping back to the beginning, going to a website, etc.

Fade Out on Last Slide: Select this option to have the last frame of your movie fade out to white.

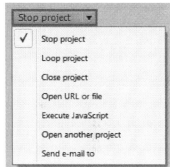

Reporting Settings

If you want to publish your movie to a learning management system (LMS) and have it track usage on the course, you need to configure the **Reporting** settings based on the needs of your LMS.

Once the settings are made, you will need to publish your project using the **Flash(SWF)** option with **Export to HTML** and **Zip Files** checked.

 Flash (SWF) Publishing, p. 209

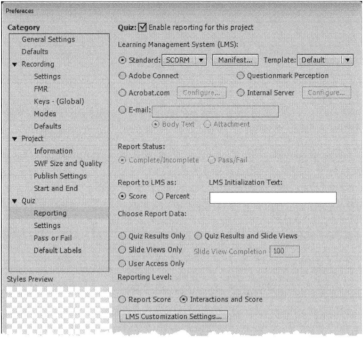

Learning Management System (LMS):

Standard: Select this option if you want to publish to a SCORM- or AICC-compliant LMS. Select the standard you want from the drop-down menu.

Manifest: Click this button to provide details about the movie, such as title, description, and length.

Template: Select an option from the menu to indicate when the data is sent to the LMS. Select **Default** to send data with every student interaction, **Custom** to configure your own settings, and **StartTrackingDataAtEnd** to send data when the user closes the movie.

Alternate Platforms: If you are publishing your course to Adobe Connect, Questionmark Perception, Acrobat.com, or an internal server, select the option for that platform. For Acrobat.com and internal servers, click the **Configure** button to enter additional details.

E-mail: If you want to e-mail the tracking data, select this option, enter the e-mail address to send it to, and indicate if you want the data in the body of the e-mail or as an attachment.

Report Status: Indicate if you want to send **Complete** and **Incomplete** or **Pass** and **Fail** as your status options. Your LMS may require one set or the other.

Report to LMS as: Indicate if you want to send the raw score (number of points) or the percent.

LMS Initialization Text: Type the text you'd like to have appear to the student while the course is opening.

Choose Report Data: Indicate which set of information you want to track. If you select slide views only, indicate what percentage of slides need to be viewed in order for the course to be considered complete.

Reporting Level: Indicate if you want to send just the score or the score as well as the interactions.

 BRIGHT IDEA

What are SCORM and AICC?

SCORM and AICC are two industry standards that govern interoperability between a course and an LMS. Basically, they ensure that the two can "talk" to each other.

Both standards are commonly used in the industry. Find out from your LMS provider which standard they use so that you can publish your movie accordingly. They may also have suggestions about what other settings work best for their LMS.

When integrating with an LMS for the first time, it is best to conduct a test early to make sure everything works properly.

 CAUTION

If you use the e-mail option, be sure to test it thoroughly. Security settings and other settings on your servers and on your users' computers may prevent this option from working.

LMS Customization Settings

Never Send Resume Data: Most LMSs offer bookmarking, which keeps track of where the students left off and asks them if they want to resume from that spot. If you check this box, Captivate will not send information about where the students leave off.

Escape Version and Session ID: This option converts the version and session ID to its URL encoded values, which is sometimes necessary for AICC publishing. For example, certain LMSs might have issues if there are special characters in the title name.

Don't Escape Characters: If you use the **Escape Version** option, use this field to enter any characters that should not be used.

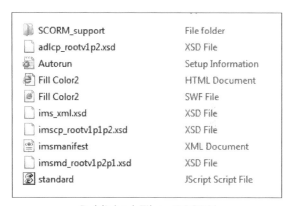

Published Files: SCORM

Publish Your Project

To publish your project:

1. Configure any publish-related settings.
2. Click the **File** menu.
3. Select **Publish**.
4. Select the publish format you want down the right-hand side.
5. Change the publishing settings, as needed.
6. Click **Publish**.

You will learn about the publish formats and publish settings on the following pages.

Flash (SWF) Publishing Options

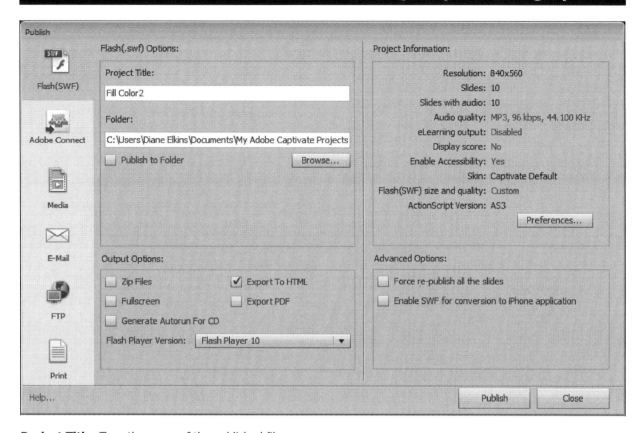

Project Title: Type the name of the published file.

Folder: Click the **Browse** button to find and select the location for the published files.

Publish to Folder: Check this box if you want Captivate to create a separate folder for your published files.

Output Options

Zip Files: Check this box if you want your published files to be zipped up into a .zip compressed folder. This is useful if you are uploading your files to a learning management system (LMS).

Fullscreen: This option includes HTML files that cause the browser window to open up to its maximum size and hide browser elements such as the toolbar and **Favorites** bar.

Generate Autorun For CD: If you check this box (only available if you have **Export to HTML** selected), the published files include a setup file that autoruns the movie on a CD. That way, when a student puts the CD into his or her computer, the published files run automatically.

Flash Player Version: You can select the version of Flash player needed to view the project.

Export to HTML: This option, checked by default, creates an HTML page and a JavaScript file to play the SWF file in the HTML page. Uncheck it if you only want the SWF file. HTML may be necessary based on how you will display the course. For example, to upload the movie to your LMS, you need the HTML file. If you are embedding the SWF on an intranet page, then you may not.

Export PDF: Check this option to create a PDF document that plays the SWF file. The PDF is a great way to send your movie via e-mail.

DESIGN TIP

Which Flash player should you pick?

Selecting an older version increases the likelihood that your users will have the necessary player. Selecting a newer version increases the likelihood that your movie will be compatible with newer platforms, such as mobile devices. Select the highest possible version that you know will work for your target audience.

Flash (SWF) Publishing Options (continued)

Project Information

For any of the information shown in blue in the dialog box, you can click the setting information to make changes.

Rescale a Project, p. 197
Audio Compression, p. 203
Reporting Features, p. 206
Project Skin, p. 198
Output Quality, p. 203

Resolution: This read-only field shows the size of the published file. Your output is always the same size as your project.

Audio Quality: This field displays the audio quality output options.

eLearning Output: This field displays the settings for connecting with a learning management system.

Display Score: If you have a quiz in your project, this field indicates whether the score will be shown to the student.

Enable Accessibility: By checking this option, Captivate activates the various accessibility options that can make a course Section 508 compatible. The course will only be accessible, however, if you set up the individual elements of the course properly, such as closed captioning.

Skin: The skin refers to the player frame that may include playback controls, a border, and a table of contents. You can change the skin settings from the **Project** menu.

Flash(SWF) Size and Quality: Click this link to change the settings for the quality of any full-motion recordings, image quality (slide backgrounds), and audio.

ActionScript Version: Captivate 5.5 publishes to ActionScript 3.

Preferences Button: Click this button to go to the **Preferences** dialog box that lets you change these and other settings.

Advanced Options

Force Re-Publish All the Slides: For any publish after the initial publish, Captivate detects what has changed and re-publishes only the slides that have changed. Check this box if you want to republish everything instead.

Enable SWF for conversion to iPhone Application: Because SWF files do not play on iOS devices such as the iPhone and iPad (at the time this book was published), this option was added for iOS compatible publishing. The relationship between Flash and iOS devices changes regularly. Please refer to the Adobe website for the latest information.

Published Files: Export to HTML

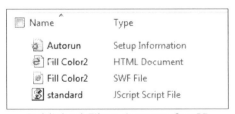

Published Files: Autorun for CD

Name	Type
Fill Color2	HTML Document
Fill Color2	SWF File
Fill Color2_fs	HTML Document
standard	JScript Script File

Published Files: Fullscreen

Published Files: Export PDF

Other Publishing Options

Adobe Connect

Use this option if you plan to upload your published movie to Adobe Connect.

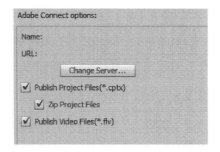

Media

The media options let you publish your project in formats other than SWF: MP4, EXE (executable for Windows), and APP (executable for Mac). For example, MP4 video files work well in iOS environments where Flash output does not work.

When publishing to MP4, additional options appear that let you select the platform you'll be using it for (such as iPad, YouTube, etc.). Making this selection optimizes the output size for the platform you are using. YouTube publishing is also available from the **File** menu.

When creating an EXE file, you can designate your own icon to appear in the taskbar, Windows Explorer, and other locations. Refer to the Captivate user manual for details about what is needed.

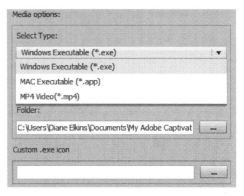

 CAUTION

Only use MP4 if your project is non-interactive. Any interactivity will be lost when publishing to this format.

E-Mail

This option lets you publish to a number of formats and automatically add them as an attachment to an e-mail. Once the files are generated, your default e-mail program opens a message with the files for you to address and send.

FTP

You can use this option to publish your file and send it directly to a website via FTP (File Transfer Protocol). You can publish to SWF, EXE, or APP formats, or instead send XML files or your project files (.cptx).

Publishing to Print/Microsoft Word

When you publish to print, you create Word documents that can be used as handouts, storyboards, job aids, etc.

Export Range: Specify which slides you want to include in the output.

Type: Select the format you want from the drop-down menu. The options in the bottom half of the panel vary based on the format you select.

Handouts: Create a format similar to the handouts in PowerPoint where you can specify the number of slides per page and then include either the slide notes or blank lines for notetaking.

Lesson: Create a document with the background image, text caption, image of anything covered by a highlight box, as well as the questions and answers for any quizzes.

Step-by-Step: Create a job aid that lists all the steps (caption text) and images of the feature highlighted (for example, just the **OK** button). Use the automatic highlight box feature during capture if you want to create a job aid like this.

Storyboard: Create a document to help you manage production. It includes slide count, preferences, and settings for the whole project as well as slide-specific information such as timing, audio, and objects.

Options:

Project Title:

Fill Color 2-HTML Background

Folder:

C:\Users\Diane Elkins\Documents\My Adobe Captivate Pro

Browse...

Export range:

(•) All   ( ) Current Slide...   ( ) Selection

( ) Slide range

Enter the slide numbers and/or slide ranges. For example, 1,3,5-12.

Type:

Handouts

Comments:

The Handout output converts your Adobe Captivate project into a Handout showing all the slides as they would appear with the chosen options.

Handout Layout Options:

[✓] Use table in the output

Slides per page   1

[ ] Caption Text
[ ] Add blank line for notes
[ ] Slide notes
[ ] Include hidden slides
[ ] Include mouse path
[ ] Include objects and questions
[ ] Include question pool slides

Note: Objects include captions, image, etc.

Appendix A

In addition to the cool tools found here in the Appendix, be sure to check out the additional tools on this book's companion website:

www.e-learninguncovered.com.

In this chapter:

- Accessibility
- Tips for Using Captivate for Mac
- Menus for Mac
- Menus for PC
- Keyboard Shortcuts
- System Variables

Notes

Accessibility

Accessibility in e-learning refers to making courses compatible with various assistive technology devices used by people with disabilities. There are three main classes of disability that affect e-learning: visual, auditory, and motor.

Impairment	Common Assistive Devices	Considerations for E-Learning
Visual Low vision No vision Color blindness	Screen readers that read information about what is happening on-screen to the user. Refreshable braille displays that create dynamic braille descriptions of what is happening on screen. Screen magnifiers that enlarge all or part of what is happening on screen.	In order for screen readers and braille displays to describe what is happening on screen, they need to be "told." Therefore, you'll need to add descriptive text, known as "alt text" to course elements for these assistive devices to read. Be sure that there are no elements that require recognition of color. Color can be used, as long as it is not the only way to tell what something means. For example, you can include a green check and a red X to indicate right or wrong, because the check and the X alone can convey the meaning. But a red and green dot would not work, since the student would need to distinguish between the colors to determine meaning. Use strong value contrast (light vs. dark) so those with low vision or color blindness can recognize on-screen elements. For example, a light blue caption on a light background may be hard for those with vision challenges to read. Vision is required in order to use a mouse properly. Visually impaired students generally do not use a mouse, instead relying on keyboard navigation through their screen reader. Therefore, course elements must be keyboard-accessible.
Auditory Hard of hearing Deafness	Closed captioning systems	For individuals with auditory impairments, it is necessary to provide a transcript of any important audio elements in the course. For static content, this can be done with a static transcript text box. For multimedia content timed to audio, the captions should also be timed to audio.
Mobility Limited dexterity No manual skills	Alternate navigation devices such as keyboards, joysticks, trackballs, and even breathing devices	For those with limited mobility, be sure that any interactive element (such as a button) is large enough for someone with rough motor skills to use. Make sure all course elements are keyboard accessible. If a course is keyboard accessible, then it will work with most other mobility-assistive devices.

Another factor to consider is cognitive impairments such as learning disabilities or dislexia. Courses are more accessible to those with cognitive impairments when there are no time constraints. For example, you can include play/pause/rewind controls and avoid timed elements such as a timed test.

Accessibility Requirements and Guidelines

There are two main reasons to make your courses accessible:

1. You want to your courses to be available for those in your target audience who may have a disability.
2. You may be required by law.

Internationally, the World Wide Web Consortium (W3C) provides web content accessibility guidelines. In addition, many countries have their own standards and requirements. In the United States, Section 508 of the Rehabilitation Act of 1973 (and later ammended) requires that information technology (including e-learning) used by the federal government be accessible to those with disabilities. Many other organizations choose to adopt that standard on their own. Go to www.section508.gov for more detailed information on the standards and the requirements.

Steps for Creating a Section 508-Compliant Project in Captivate

The following pages contain the accessibility standards for web pages from the Section 508 requirements for web-based intranet and internet information and applications, along with the corresponding procedures in Captivate.

This guide is not intended to be a stand-alone guide, but rather to be used in conjunction with other educational resources (such as www.section508.gov) and thorough accessibility testing.

Section 508 - 1194.22

(a) A text equivalent for every non-text element shall be provided (e.g., via "alt", "longdesc", or in element content).

- In order for alt text to be published with a movie, you must first enable accessibility in the project's preferences.
- Add alt text to each slide that conveys content.
- Add alt text to each object that conveys content. For example, if you have an image of a diagram, you'll need to add a text description of that diagram for screen readers to read.

 Change Publish Settings, p. 204
Slide Properties, p. 35
Object Information, p. 89

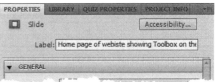

(b) Equivalent alternatives for any multimedia presentation shall be synchronized with the presentation.

Add closed captioning timed to audio (if audio is used) or add caption objects timed to audio.

 Closed Captioning, p. 80
Timing Slide Objects, p. 105

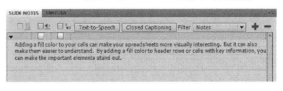

(c) Web pages shall be designed so that all information conveyed with color is also available without color, for example from context or markup.

This is done through your own design of the course. Avoid any element in which color is the only way of communicating information. As a test, print out screens in grayscale to determine if the course elements can still be understood.

(d) Documents shall be organized so they are readable without requiring an associated style sheet.

(e) Redundant text links shall be provided for each active region of a server-side image map.

(f) Client-side image maps shall be provided instead of server-side image maps except where the regions cannot be defined with an available geometric shape.

Captivate does not use style sheets or image maps, so these standards are not applicable.

(g) Row and column headers shall be identified for data tables.

(h) Markup shall be used to associate data cells and header cells for data tables that have two or more logical levels of row or column headers.

Captivate does not have an option for tables. If you create a table elsewhere and bring it in as a graphic, be sure to provide detailed alt text for the content in the table.

(i) Frames shall be titled with text that facilitates frame identification and navigation.

Captivate does not use frames, so this part of the standard is not applicable for a Captivate project.

Steps for 508-Compliance (continued)

(j) Pages shall be designed to avoid causing the screen to flicker with a frequency greater than 2 Hz and lower than 55 Hz.

Anything that flashes or flickers needs to be either slower than 2 times per second or faster than 55 times per second. Anything in between that range could cause seizures in some people. If you incorporate text animations, check to see how quickly any elements flash. Plus, if you import animations, animated gifs, videos, or use show/hide actions to make something flash, make sure you work outside of the prohibited range.

(k) A text-only page, with equivalent information or functionality, shall be provided to make a web site comply with the provisions of this part, when compliance cannot be accomplished in any other way. The content of the text-only page shall be updated whenever the primary page changes.

You can provide text equivalents through closed captioning, caption text, or links to a document. You can link to a document using the **Open URL/File action**. Just be sure that the document in question is also accessible.

 Action Types, p. 219

(l) When pages utilize scripting languages to display content, or to create interface elements, the information provided by the script shall be identified with functional text that can be read by assistive technology.

This standard means that in addition to the alt text you set up as part of (a), system controls need to be understandable by screen readers and accessible using keyboard navigation. When you enable accessibility for the project (a), it converts the buttons and other interface/navigation features to be accessible. However, there are a few features that are not accessible that cannot be used in a 508-compliant course. In a quiz, you can only use multiple choice, true/false, and rating scale question types. The other types of questions are not accessible.

(m) When a web page requires that an applet, plug-in or other application be present on the client system to interpret page content, the page must provide a link to a plug-in or applet that complies with §1194.21(a) through (l).

Be sure to include links to the Adobe Flash Player BEFORE the student launches the course. (If they don't have the Flash player, they cannot access a Captivate page with the link!) Also, be sure to provide links to Acrobat Reader and any other plug-ins required to view content.

(n) When electronic forms are designed to be completed on-line, the form shall allow people using assistive technology to access the information, field elements, and functionality required for completion and submission of the form, including all directions and cues.

When creating forms to capture information from a student, be sure to use only use accessible options. Use buttons; multiple-choice, true/false, and rating scale questions; and text entry boxes. Do not use other question types.

(o) A method shall be provided that permits users to skip repetitive navigation links.

If someone visits multiple web pages, they have to listen to (with a screen reader) and/or tab through (with keyboard navigation) all the main navigational elements each time they visit a new page. This standard requires that a link be provided that lets the user skip these items that appear on every page.

(p) When a timed response is required, the user shall be alerted and given sufficient time to indicate more time is required.

Avoid using a timed test unless there is a job-specific reason for the timing. If you do use a timed test or add/build any content with a time limit, be sure to build in an extension system.

Accessibility Design Considerations

Accessibility can be defined in many different ways. The accessibility guidelines are subject to interpretation, and there is much debate about what makes a course usable and compliant. Therefore, it is extremely important that you carefully evaluate the standards and guidance provided by the government, accessibility groups, and your own organization (legal, HR, I.T., etc.) to determine what accessibility means for your organization.

Here are some additional tips to help make your courses more accessible and more usable to those with disabilities.

- There is no substitute for thorough testing. Be sure to test your designs with accessibility devices to make sure they work as planned.

- Add project information. The data found in the **Project Information** panel is read by screen readers, so be sure to enter your data there.

 Project Information, p. 202

- Give screen reader students full control over the audio. If the audio plays automatically and the screen reader is reading slide information, the student may not be able to understand what is happening.

- Consider the order that the objects will be read by a screen reader. Screen readers read objects from right to left and from top to bottom. Use a logical order so that the screen reader student will understand what is happening on the screen. If you'd like more flexibility, search online for a tab order widget that gives you more control over the order.

- When adding buttons or other interactive objects, don't just call them buttons in the alt text. Provide a description of what the buttons do.

- Captivate lets you use a larger-than-normal mouse cursor in your projects. This can be helpful for those with low vision.

 Double Mouse Size, p. 130

- Remember that, by default, the closed caption button is NOT included on the playbar. If you are using captions, be sure to enable the **CC** button, or create your own logic using advanced actions.

 Configure Project Skin, p. 198

- Be careful about assigning keyboard shortcuts to interactive objects such as buttons. Those shortcuts might conflict with the shortcuts that a screen reader uses.

- Make sure any elements you add to your course—such as animations, widgets, or JavaScript commands—are accessible as well.

- If you are teaching computer procedures, consider very carefully what the best design is for students using assistive devices. For example, is the software you are teaching accessible? And, would someone using assistive technology be using the software the same way as someone who is not? Consider creating separate courses based on how the student will be accessing the software being taught.

Tips for Using Captivate for Macintosh

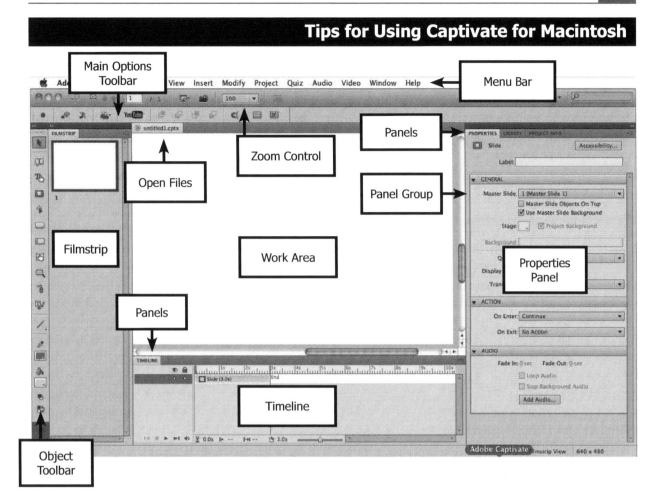

Interface & Navigation

The Mac interface is very similar to the PC interface. Key differences include:

- The toolbars are arranged slightly differently, with fewer buttons on the Main Options toolbar.
- In most dialog boxes for the PC, **OK** (or similar) is on the left and **Cancel** is on the right. They are usually switched on the Mac.
- Right-click commands on the PC are control-click commands on a Mac.
- The **Preferences** dialog box is on the **Adobe Captivate** menu instead of the **Edit** menu.

Many of the keyboard shortcuts are the same between Mac and PC. The one major exception is that you would use the **Command** key instead of the **Control** key. See page 224 for commonly-used shortcuts.

Publishing

If you want your movie to play on an iOS device, you can use the MP4 format. This works with non-interactive movies. You can create a Mac-compatible executable using the the .app publish format. See pages 178 and 211.

Please note: This is not intended to be a comprehensive list of differences between Captivate for Mac and Captivate for PC. While most of the capabilities between the two will be the same, you may encounter some differences.

Captivate for Mac Menus

Adobe Captivate | File | Edit

About Adobe Captivate...

Preferences... ⌘,

Services ▶

Hide Adobe Captivate ⌘H
Hide Others ⌥⌘H
Show All

Quit Adobe Captivate ⌘Q

File | Edit View Insert Mo

New Project ▶
Record new project... ⌘R
Open... ⌘O
Browse in Bridge
Open Recent ▶
Close ⌘W
Close All ⌥⇧W

Save ⌘S
Save As... ⌥⇧⌘S
Save All

Import ▶
Collaborate ▶

Export ▶

Publish... ⌥⇧F12
Publish To YouTube...
Publish Settings...
Preview ▶

Project Info...

Edit | View Insert Modify Project Q

Undo Insert Audio Resources ⌘Z
Redo ⌘Y

Cut ⌘X
Copy ⌘C
Copy Background ⇧⌘Y
Paste ⌘V
Paste as Background ⌥⇧V

Duplicate ⌘D
Delete ⌫
Select All ⌘A

Find Background in the Library ⌥⌘F
Find and Replace ⌘F

Edit with Microsoft PowerPoint ▶
Edit PSD Source File

Edit Points ⌥⌘E
Edit Gradient ⇧⌘G
Edit Text F2

Object Style Manager... ⇧F7

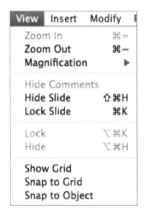

View | Insert Modify F

Zoom In ⌘=
Zoom Out ⌘−
Magnification ▶

Hide Comments
Hide Slide ⇧⌘H
Lock Slide ⌘K

Lock ⌥⌘K
Hide ⌥⌘H

Show Grid
Snap to Grid
Snap to Object

Insert | Modify Project Quiz

New Slide ⇧⌘V
Blank Slide ⇧⌘J
PowerPoint Slide... ⇧⌘P
Question Slide... ⇧Q
Recording Slide... ⌥⌘O
Image Slide... ⇧⌘S
Animation Slide... ⇧⌘N

Master Slide ⌥⌘M

Standard Objects ▶

Placeholder Objects ▶
Placeholder Slides ▶

Slide Video... ⌥⌘V

Image... ⇧⌘M
Animation... ⇧⌘A
FLV or F4V File... ⇧⌘F
Text Animation ⇧⌘X
Widget... ⇧⌘W

Slide Transition ▶

Modify | Project Quiz Audio Vide

Rescale project...

Redraw Shape ⌥⌘W

Arrange ▶
Align ▶

Move Question to ▶

Merge with the background ⌘M
Merge FMR Slides

Sync with Playhead ⌘L
Show for the rest of the slide ⌘E

Increase Indent ⌘I
Decrease Indent ⇧⌘I

Auto-adjust Rollover Area ⌥⌘R

Update from Source

Mouse ▶

Group ▶

Captivate for Mac Menus

Project Quiz Audio Video

Advanced Actions...	⇧⌘F9
Variables...	
Table of Contents...	⇧⌘F10
Skin Editor...	⇧⌘F11
Advanced Interaction	⌘F9
Check Spelling...	F7

Quiz Audio Video Window He

Question Slide...	⇧Q
Random Question Slide	⌥⇧R
Import Question Pools...	
Question Pool Manager...	⌥⇧Q
Quiz Preferences...	
Download Quiz Templates	

Audio Video Window Help

Import to	▶
Record to	▶
Edit	▶
Remove	▶
Audio Management...	⌥⇧A
Speech Management...	⌥⇧S
Settings...	

Video Window Help

Insert Slide Video...	⌥⌘V
Edit Video Timing...	
Video Management...	

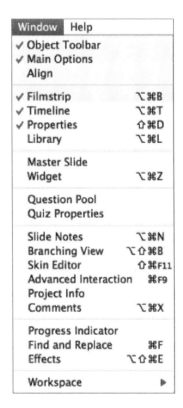

Window Help

✓ Object Toolbar	
✓ Main Options	
Align	
✓ Filmstrip	⌥⌘B
✓ Timeline	⌥⌘T
✓ Properties	⇧⌘D
Library	⌥⌘L
Master Slide	
Widget	⌥⌘Z
Question Pool	
Quiz Properties	
Slide Notes	⌥⌘N
Branching View	⌥⇧⌘B
Skin Editor	⇧⌘F11
Advanced Interaction	⌘F9
Project Info	
Comments	⌥⌘X
Progress Indicator	
Find and Replace	⌘F
Effects	⌥⇧⌘E
Workspace	▶

Help

Search

Adobe Captivate Help	F1
Adobe Product Improvement Program...	
Adobe Captivate Blog	
Product Registration...	
Deactivate...	
Updates...	
Access Adobe Resources...	

Captivate for PC Menus

Web Resource:
Menu, Toolbars, & Shortcuts

Captivate for PC Menus (continued)

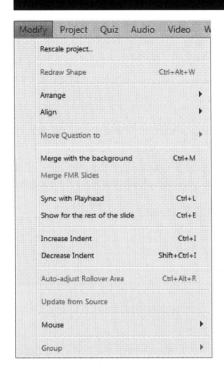

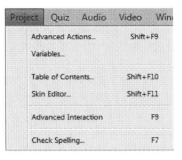

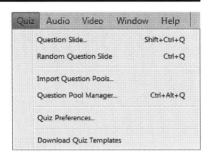

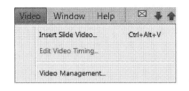

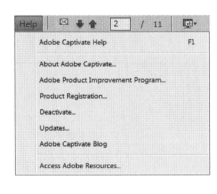

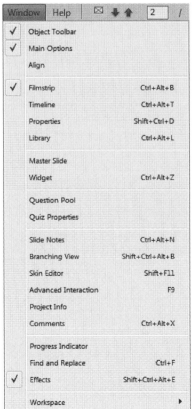

Useful Keyboard Shortcuts

There are over a hundred keyboard shortcuts in Captivate, all of which can be found in the Adobe Captivate 5.5 Help documentation. Here is a list of the shortcuts that the authors find most useful to memorize.

	PC	**Mac**
Insert		
New Slide	Shift + Ctrl + V	Shift + Cmd + V
Blank Slide	Shift + Ctrl + J	Shift + Cmd + J
Question Slide	Shift + Ctrl + Q	Shift + Q
Text Caption	Shift + Ctrl + C	Shift + Cmd + C
Mouse	Shift + Ctrl + U	Shift + Cmd + U
Editing		
Undo	Ctrl + Z	Cmd + Z
Redo	Ctrl + Y	Cmd + Y
Cut	Ctrl + X	Cmd + X
Copy	Ctrl + C	Cmd + C
Paste	Ctrl + V	Cmd + V
Duplicate	Ctrl + D	Cmd + D
File Management		
Save	Ctrl + S	Cmd + S
Publish	Shift + F12	Option + Shift + F12
Formatting		
Bold	Ctrl + B	Cmd + B
Underline	Ctrl + U	Cmd + U
Italics	Ctrl + I	Cmd + I
Timing		
Sync Object to Playhead	Ctrl + L	Cmd + L
Show for Rest of Slide	Ctrl + E	Cmd + E
Start Next Slide (in Edit Slides Audio)	Ctrl + S	Cmd + S
Play/Preview		
Play Slide	F3	F3
Preview Project	F4	F4
Preview From This Slide	F8	Cmd + F8
Preview Next 5 Slides	F10	Cmd + F10
Preview In Web Browser	F12	Cmd + F12
Toggle Play/Pause	Space	Space
View		
Zoom In	Ctrl + =	Cmd + =
Zoom Out	Ctrl + -	Cmd + -

Default recording shortcuts for PC

General:
To Stop Recording: End
To Pause/Resume Recording: Pause

Manual Recording:
To Capture a Screenshot: Print Screen

Full Motion Recording:
To Start Full Motion Recording: F9
To Stop Full Motion Recording: F10

Panning:
For Automatic Panning: F4
For Manual Panning: F3
To Stop Panning: F7
To snap recording window to mouse: F11
To toggle mouse capture in FMR: F12

Default recording shortcuts for Mac

General:
To Stop Recording: Cmd-Enter
To Pause/Resume Recording: Cmd-F2

Manual Recording:
To Capture a Screenshot: Cmd-F6

Full Motion Recording:
To Start Full Motion Recording: Cmd-F9
To Stop Full Motion Recording: Cmd-F10

Panning:
For Automatic Panning: Cmd-F4
For Manual Panning: Cmd-F3
To Stop Panning: Cmd-F7
To snap recording window to mouse: Cmd-F11
To toggle mouse capture in FMR: Cmd-F12

Web Resource:
Menu, Toolbars, & Shortcuts

System Variables

Variable	Definition	Default	Comments
Movie Control			
cpCmndCC	Enable/Disable Closed Captioning. Set value to 1 to display closed captions.	0	You can add a closed captioning button to the Playback Control bar. Or you can add your own buttons or logic by setting this variable to 1 vs. 0.
cpCmndGotoSlide	Assign the slide number that the movie should move to before pausing. Index begins with zero.	-1	
cpCmndMute	Mute the audio. Set to 1 to mute and 0 to unmute.	0	You can add an audio on/off button to the playbar. Or, you can add your own buttons or logic by setting this variable to 1 vs. 0.
cpCmndPlaybarMoved	Set to 1 if the playbar has moved.	0	
cpCmndShowPlaybar	Provides information about the visibility of the playbar. Returns 1 if the playbar is visible, else 0.	1	
cpCmndVolume	Control the movie's volume. Value can range from 0 to 100.	50	You can change volume throughout the movie or create a control that lets the student do it.
cpLockTOC	Enable/disable user interaction on TOC. Set to 1 to disable.	0	You may want the student to be able to move around freely except in a quiz. You can add an action at the beginning of the quiz that disables the ability to move around.
rdcmndExit	Exit the movie. Set to 1 to exit.	0	You can add an exit button to the Playback Control bar. Or, you can add your own button or logic by setting this variable to 1.
rdcmndGotoFrame-AndResume	Assign to this variable the frame number to jump to and play. Index begins with zero.	-1	Use this to jump to a specific part of a slide. Calculate the frame number you need by multiplying the number of seconds of the point you want to jump to by the frames per second of the movie (usually 30).
rdcmndNextSlide	Go to the next slide. Set 1 to jump to next slide	0	
rdcmndPause	Pause the movie. Set to 1 to pause.	0	You can add a pause button to the Playback Control bar. Or, you can add your own buttons or logic by setting this variable to 1. Use the rdcmdResume variable to unpause.
rdcmndPrevious	Go to the previous slide. Set 1 to jump to previous slide	0	
rdcmndResume	Resume the movie. Set to 1 to resume.	0	If the movie is paused, create a button or logic to unpause it by setting this varable to 1.

Variables, p. 139

System Variables (continued)

Variable	Definition	Default	Comments
Movie Information			
CaptivateVersion	Current version of Captivate	v5.5.0	
cpInfoCurrentSlide	Current slide number. Index begins with 1.	N/A	Use this to display a page counter to the student.
cpInfoCurrentSlideLabel	Name of the Current Slide	N/A	Use this to automatically display the name of the slide to the student.
cpInfoCurrentSlideType	Type of the slide that plays now. This can be Normal Slide, Question Slide, or Random Question Slide.	Normal	Use this information for if/then logic based on slide type. For example, enable TOC navigation on normal slides but disable it on quiz slides.
cpInfoElapsedTimeMS	Time elapsed (in milliseconds) since the movie started playing.	0	
cpInfoHasPlaybar	Provides information about the visibility of the playbar. Returns 1 if the playbar is visible, else 0.	1	Use this to create a toggle to show or hide the toolbar. Add a show action if this is 0 and a hide action if this is 1.
cpInfoIsStandalone	This value would be set to 1 when published as .exe or .app. Otherwise, it is set to 0	1	
cpInfoLastVisitedSlide	The slide last visited. Index begins with zero.	0	Use this information to create a Return button.
cpInfoPrevSlide	The previous slide	-1	Use this information to create a Back button.
rdinfoCurrentFrame	The current frame number. Index begins with zero	1	
rdinfoCurrentSlide	The current slide number. Index begins with zero	1	Use this for a page counter
rdinfoFPS	Frame rate of the movie in fps (frames per second)	30	
rdinfoFrameCount	Number of frames in the project.	1	
rdinfoSlideCount	Number of slides in the project.	1	Use this for a page counter that includes the total number of slides (e.g., 4 of 10).

System Variables (continued)

Variable	Definition	Default	Comments
Movie Metadata			
cpInfoAuthor	Name of the Author	N/A	Pulls information from the **Project Information** tab in **Preferences**.
cpInfoCompany	Name of the Company	N/A	
cpInfoCopyright	Copyright Info	N/A	
cpInfoCourseID	ID of the Course	-1	
cpInfoCourseName	Name of the Course		
cpInfoDescription	Description of the Project		Pulls information from the **Project Information** tab in **Preferences**.
cpInfoEmail	E-mail Address		
cpInfoProjectName	Name of the Adobe Captivate Project		
cpInfoWebsite	URL of the company website, starting with www.		
System Information			
cpInfoCurrentDate	Current Date: Date set on user's computer	Format: dd	Use the date information to display on a certificate or to create your own expiration feature.
cpInfoCurrentDateString	Current Date in the Format mm/dd/yyyy	Format: mm/dd/ yyyy	
cpInfoCurrentDay	Current Day	Format: 1	
cpInfoCurrentHour	Current Hour: Hour set on user's computer	Format: hh	
cpInfoCurrentMinutes	Current Minutes: Minutes set on user's computer	Format: mm	
cpInfoCurrentMonth	Current Month: Month set on user's computer	Format: mm	
cpInfoCurrentTime	Current Time in the Format hh:mm:ss	Format: hh:mm:ss	
cpInfoCurrentYear	Current Year: Year set on user's computer	Format: yyyy	
cpInfoEpochMS	Time elapsed, in milliseconds, since January 01, 1970.	0	

System Variables (continued)

Variable	Definition	Default	Comments
Quizzing			
cpInfoPercentage	Scoring in Percentage	0	Tracks the quiz score in percent form.
cpQuizInfoAnswerChoice	Chosen Answer		Tracks the student's answer to the current question. Use for conditional logic based on the student's answer, such as option-specific feedback.
cpQuizInfoAttempts	Number of times the quiz has been attempted	0	Use this for conditional logic, such as showing different feedback captions based on whether it is the first or second attempt.
cpQuizInfoLastSlidePointScored	Score for last quiz slide	0	Shows how many points were gained for the previous slide.
cpQuizInfoMaxAttempts OnCurrentQuestion	Maximum attempts on the current question	0	Use this to set up custom maximum attempts logic.
cpQuizInfoPassFail	Quiz Result	0	Use for conditional logic or to display to the students whether they passed or failed a quiz.
cpQuizInfoPointsPer QuestionSlide	Points for the question slide	0	Use to show the student how many points are at stake for the current question.
cpQuizInfoPointsscored	Points scored in the project	0	Use for conditional logic or to display to the students their current number of points.
cpQuizInfoQuestionSlideTiming	Time limit in seconds for the current question.	0	Use to display to the student the amount of time available if there is a limit.
cpQuizInfoQuestionSlideType	Question Slide Type. For example, Multiple-Choice or True-False.	choice	
cpQuizInfoQuizPassPercent	Passing percentage for the quiz	80	Use to display to the student the score (as a percentage) required to pass the quiz.
cpQuizInfoQuizPassPoints	Passing points for the quiz	0	Use to display to the student the score (as a raw points) required to pass the quiz.
cpQuizInfoTotalCorrectAnswers	Number of Correct Answers	0	Use to show the student the number of answers the student has answered correctly.
cpQuizInfoTotalProjectPoints	Total project points	0	
cpQuizInfoTotalQuestions PerProject	Number of Questions per Project	0	
cpQuizInfoTotalQuizPoints	Total Quiz Points	0	
cpQuizInfoTotalUnanswered Questions	Number of Unanswered Questions	0	

Index i

Visit the companion site at:

www.e-learninguncovered.com

Resources for Rapid Developers

1. Download free resources
2. Access practice files
3. Sign up for our blog
4. Ask about bulk purchases
5. Explore the other books in the series

E-Learning Uncovered
is brought to you by:

Custom E-Learning Development

E-Learning Consulting

E-Learning Team Training

Specializing in:

Articulate, Captivate, Lectora,

and Other Rapid

Development Tools

www.artisanelearning.com

info@artisanelearning.com

(904) 254-2494

Made in the USA
Lexington, KY
17 May 2014